THE LIFE HISTORY OF THE UNITED STATES

Volume 6: 1861-1876

THE UNION RESTORED

TIME LIFE BOOKS ®

THE LIFE HISTORY OF THE UNITED STATES

Consulting Editor, Henry F. Graff

Volume 6: 1861-1876

THE UNION RESTORED

by T. Harry Williams

and the Editors of

TIME-LIFE BOOKS

TIME-LIFE BOOKS, NEW YORK

TIME-LIFE BOOKS

FOUNDER: Henry R. Luce 1898-1967

Editor-in-Chief: Hedley Donovan
Chairman of the Board: Andrew Heiskell
President: James R. Shepley
Chairman, Executive Committee: James A. Linen
Group Vice President: Rhett Austell

Vice Chairman: Roy E. Larsen

MANAGING EDITOR: Jerry Korn
Assistant Managing Editors: David Maness,
Martin Mann, A. B. C. Whipple
Planning Director: Oliver E. Allen
Art Director: Sheldon Cotler
Chief of Research: Beatrice T. Dobie
Director of Photography: Melvin L. Scott
Senior Text Editor: Diana Hirsh
Assistant Art Director: Arnold C. Holeywell

PUBLISHER: Joan D. Manley
General Manager: John D. McSweeney
Business Manager: John Steven Maxwell
Sales Director: Carl G. Jaeger
Promotion Director: Paul R. Stewart
Public Relations Director: Nicholas Benton

THE LIFE HISTORY OF THE UNITED STATES

Editorial Staff for Volume 6
SERIES EDITOR: Sam Welles
Designer: Douglas R. Steinbauer
Staff Writers: Gerald Simons, Alfred Lansing,
Jonathan Kastner, Edmund White,
Paul Trachtman
Chief Researcher: Clara E. Nicolai
Researchers: Jean Snow, Terry Drucker,
Malabar Brodeur, Jacqueline Coates,
Lilla Zabriskie, Patricia Tolles,
Madeleine Richards, Theo Pascal

EDITORIAL PRODUCTION
Production Editor: Douglas B. Graham
Assistant Production Editor: Gennaro C. Esposito
Quality Director: Robert L. Young
Assistant Quality Director: James J. Cox
Copy Staff: Rosalind Stubenberg (chief),
Florence Keith
Picture Department: Dolores A. Littles
Art Assistants: James D. Smith, Wayne R. Young

THE AUTHOR of Volumes 5 and 6 of this series, T. Harry Williams, has devoted his professional career—as teacher, writer and editor—to the history of the Civil War, on which he is a leading expert. A Northerner born in Vinegar Hill, Illinois, he has been living in the South since 1941. He earned his Ph.D. at the University of Wisconsin; since 1953 he has been Boyd Professor of History at Louisiana State University. His book *Huey Long* received the 1969 National Book Award and the Pulitzer Prize for biography. He is also the author of *Lincoln and His Generals,* a definitive work on command problems; *Lincoln and the Radicals;* and *P. G. T. Beauregard.*

THE CONSULTING EDITOR for this series, Henry F. Graff, is Professor of History at Columbia University in New York.

Valuable assistance in preparing this volume was given by Roger Butterfield, who served as picture consultant; Editorial Production, Norman Airey; Library, Benjamin Lightman; Picture Collection, Doris O'Neil; Photographic Laboratory, George Karas; TIME-LIFE News Service, Murray J. Gart. Revisions Staff: Harold C. Field, Joan Chambers.

CONTENTS

A NOTE TO THE READER: The story of the Civil War is related in two volumes of this series. Volume 5 contains accounts of the war's political events. The military events of the period are reported in this volume. —THE EDITORS

1. THAT "STRANGE SAD WAR"

THE Civil War was two wars in one. It was the first of the modern wars: big, almost total, a war of matériel and ideologies and unlimited objectives. It witnessed the introduction or the first prominent employment of such instruments of the future as mass armies, breech-loading and repeating rifles, railroads, armored ships, the telegraph, balloons, trenches and wire entanglements. It was also the last of the traditional wars—romantic, leisurely and limited. Generals still arranged battles in the style of the 18th Century, and men still charged in the mass formations that the new weapons were making obsolete. It was a war of technology and machines, and it was also a war of men, who fought sometimes with the most primitive of weapons and sometimes with their bare hands. It was a war that saw bitter hatreds aroused on both sides but that also witnessed incredible acts of chivalrous camaraderie performed by the soldiers of both armies. It was a war of conflicting ideals, and yet the two contending peoples spoke the same language and for the most part believed in the same principles and values.

Modern war and storybook war—there is no conflict quite like it in history. The poet Walt Whitman, who saw much of it, caught its rare quality in a memorable phrase. It was, he said, that "strange sad war."

When it began, in the spring of 1861, most people on both sides were confident that it would not last long. It would end quickly because the inferior enemy would not put up much of a fight. In New York City men were knocked

PRESERVER OF THE UNION, President Abraham Lincoln gazes with calm determination from this portrait by Peter Baumgras, painted during the turbulence of the war.

down on the streets for saying that perhaps the South would fight well. In Richmond a former governor of Virginia boasted that once the brave men of Dixie advanced on the Northern popinjays, the war would swiftly halt.

These predictions reflected more than an innocent cocksureness. Even leaders who should have known better thought it would be a short war. Lengthy conflicts simply were not a part of the American consciousness. There had been one long war in the national experience, the Revolution, but the two wars since had been relatively brief. At the worst, it was believed, this war would be like the one with Mexico, lasting perhaps a year or so. It would be fought, of course, with the kind of soldiers Americans had always employed—volunteers who would rush forward to offer their services.

In the first fine flush of enthusiasm it seemed that volunteering would do the job. An outburst of patriotism gripped both peoples. In the North it took on the proportions of an uprising. A New York newspaper reported that the city's people were "wild with excitement" and that "the streets were vocal with a demand for blood." Excitement and determination ran equally high in the South. The governor of Mississippi informed President Davis that so many men were coming forward that arms for them were not available. "All Mississippi is in a fever to get to the field," the governor concluded, "and hail an order to march as the greatest favor you can bestow on them."

Both governments set the same initial troop quota, 500,000 men. The North met its figure, and although the South did not, the response was heavy enough to fill its armies to a respectable size. But with an eye to the future the North within a few months began enlisting all its men for a three-year period, while most Southerners were still able to sign up for one year. As the war wore into its second year, the rude truth dawned that it was not following the prescribed script. It was not going to be a short and easy war at all, but a long and probably not a very pleasant one. Abruptly, the ardor for martial adventuring dwindled and the flow of men into the armies fell to a trickle.

A Northern cartoon prescribed this costume as appropriate "for the brave stay-at-home." But not all service dodgers stayed at home. Thousands fled to Canada or Europe; 500 crossed the border at Detroit in one day. One ship was stopped at sea and all male passengers forced back to New York.

FOR both governments the situation posed a hard fact and a crisis: This war was going to require huge aggregations of men, and the conventional democratic procedures would not raise them. The crisis was especially perilous for the South. With a free population less than one third that of the North, it had a smaller manpower reservoir to draw on: only 1,140,000 men of military age as compared to the North's four million. And in the spring of 1862 the South's emergency was dangerously immediate. The terms of the 12-month men, the veterans, were expiring and few of them showed much inclination to re-enlist. With the old hands leaving and new men not volunteering, the Confederacy faced the possibility of seeing its armies evaporate. A Georgia editor voiced something of the despair gripping Southern leaders. "Turn out or perish," he urged his compatriots, "that history may not perpetuate the damning disgrace that ten millions of freemen, for the love of money, let themselves be subjugated by twenty millions whom they pronounced cowards."

The Confederate government met the issue the only way it could be met. In April 1862 the Southern Congress enacted the first national draft law passed by an American legislative body. It provided that all white males between the ages of 18 and 35 were liable to military service for three years. The 12-month men already in service were, much to their disgust, not to be released; but they had to serve only two more years. For the moment the

Conscription Act averted the threat of a crisis. But before the end of the year Congress had to raise the upper age limit to 45, an indication of the continuing need for compulsion and of continuing manpower problems.

In 1863 the Confederacy carried its largest forces on the rolls, a total of some 500,000 men. From that peak, Rebel manpower rapidly went downhill. The loss of large chunks of territory and a developing war weariness contributed to decrease the size of the armies. As 1864 opened, probably not more than 234,000 Confederate troops were actually present for duty. In a desperate move to tap all available sources, Congress extended the lower age limit to 17 and the upper to 50. The results were meager. Men avoided the draft or deserted, and the machinery for enforcement practically broke down. At the close of 1864 only 100,000 of the once-mighty host in gray remained on the field. The last frantic effort to keep the armies up to strength came in 1865 when Congress authorized the employment of 300,000 slaves as soldiers. The war ended before this strange experiment could be set in motion.

One reason for the failure of the draft laws to raise more men was the numerous exemptions that were provided. The framers of the laws grasped the modern principle of selective service: that some men were more valuable at home than in the army, that some had, in fact, to be left at home to keep the war going. But they erred in granting too many groups occupational exemptions, in exempting people who were not necessary to the war effort, and in providing deferments that seemed like class favoritism.

Among those exempted were druggists, teachers, editors, printers and the like, as well as the more vital productive services. Many now rushed to get into the sheltered occupations. Suddenly there were more schools and drugstores than ever before. The appearance of so many "apothecaries" occasioned wide ridicule. One editor commented that most of them "could not analyze the simplest compound or put up the plainest prescription." Their only evidence of professionalism, he went on, was "a few empty jars, a cheap assortment of combs and brushes, a few bottles of 'hair dye' and 'wizard oil' and other Yankee nostrums."

The first Confederate draft act permitted any man who was called up to purchase a substitute to go in his place. This provision, copied from European practice, was intended to protect from the draft the men who directed production facilities, but it was denounced as a gesture to the rich. Similar in intent and arousing the same reaction was the provision exempting one white man on each plantation with 20 or more slaves. Of this clause one general snorted: "Some exempts claim to own 20 Negroes, and with justice might claim to be masters of an infinite amount of cowardice." Eventually substitution was abolished and the 20-slave law modified, but only after both had done serious damage to morale. Still, with all their defects, the pioneering Confederate conscription acts passed the test of performance: They mobilized a large percentage of the available manpower.

T HE Northern experience paralleled that of the South. With its larger population, over 22 million, the North could rely on volunteering longer, but eventually it too had to come to conscription. In March 1863, almost a year after the Confederacy acted, the United States Congress passed a national draft act. It provided that all able-bodied males, between the ages of 20 and 45 if unmarried and 20 and 35 if married, were liable for service of three years.

Drumming up Confederate recruits, a slave joins a young drummer and a fifer in a Southern city. Early in the war many wealthy Southerners believed that it was more honorable to volunteer in the ranks than to accept a commission. Others went in as officers accompanied by Negro servants.

Few exceptions were allowed, and almost none of an occupational nature. But any draftee could avoid service by hiring a substitute or by paying the government a $300 fee. Both loopholes aroused anger and dissatisfaction, and eventually the cash commutation was repealed—for all but conscientious objectors, who could still buy exemption.

A curious feature of the Northern draft law was that it did not directly conscript; rather, its purpose was to spur enlistments by threatening conscription. At specified times the government announced a call for troops and assigned each state a quota based on its population. The states had an opportunity to fill their quota by offering cash bounties or other inducements to men to enlist. Only if this failed did the national government step in to fill out the quota with the draft. Actually, relatively few men, about 45,000, were directly drafted, but the law had all the effect of a real draft. The states, to avoid federal intervention, went to enormous efforts to raise men, and the size of the armies increased steadily, rising to a peak in 1865.

In all, 1.5 million Northerners were brought out for three years' service. They were, despite the devious workings of conscription, drafted by national action into a national army. For Americans it was a strange new exercise of government power and it was widely resented—by poor men who could not afford to buy their way out, by recent immigrants who had experienced compulsory military service in their home countries, and by people who did not want to fight to emancipate blacks. Organized opposition was, however, rare.

The most formidable defiance occurred in July 1863 in New York City, which throughout the war remained a Democratic stronghold. Here the announcement of a draft call stirred people in the poorer quarters to wild anger that developed into rioting. For three days mobs roamed the city, fighting the police, hanging blacks and burning a Negro orphan asylum. Although Republican newspapers exaggerated the numbers of deaths and the extent of the destruction—probably 74 people were killed instead of the reported 500—the episode was serious enough. Army troops had to be moved in to restore order.

The draft riots in New York owed their violence in part to the fact that saloons were open Sundays. The draft began on a Saturday; by Monday the fury of the masses had been fueled by quantities of alcohol. Catholic priests, under Archbishop John Hughes (above), helped to quell the mobs (below).

THE men in the contending armies were largely native white Americans. Perhaps as many as a fourth of the men in the Union forces were foreign-born, but a number of these had come to the United States years before the war. Most of these alien soldiers were of German or Irish birth, and often they enlisted as units. The colorful Irish Brigade of New York City carried flags of emerald green that flaunted a harp and a shamrock. Fifteen of the 26 regiments of the 11th Corps were German; members of this corps were known throughout the army as "the Dutchmen." Approximately 180,000 blacks, most of them recently freed slaves, served in the Northern ranks as soldiers or laborers. The Southern armies, representing a more homogeneous white population than the North, included a small percentage of aliens. Still the Northern and Southern soldiers were very much alike as warriors.

The Northern armies, coming from a more diversified society, were more complex in the occupational sense; they contained more men who could do more of the things required in a modern army. The soldier-historians of a typical Ohio regiment claimed that its members could do anything from selling a paper of pins to constructing a railroad. That such talk was not mere boasting was discovered by a general in Maryland. He needed a locomotive to transport troops and found one in a station. But it had been deliberately disabled. Turning to his men, he asked if any of them knew anything about the machine. A private stepped forward and after an inspection answered: "That engine was made in our shop; I guess I can fit her up and run her." Soon the locomotive was in service.

The Southern armies, for their part, numbered more men who had natural martial qualities. Many Southerners were accustomed to horses almost from birth, and they easily became superb cavalrymen. And coming from a more simple society, the Southern soldiers took to fighting with more zest and fury than did the Northerners. Whereas to the Northerner, war was a vexatious interruption of the routine of life, it was to many a Southerner a sheer joy. And the values of Southern life—the cavalier and the martial traditions—imparted to Southern men a conviction that often enabled the Gray ranks to attempt, and sometimes to accomplish, the impossible—to swing up the slopes of Cemetery Ridge in a sheet of fire, to stand for weeks in the bitter trenches of Vicksburg, and to win from an admiring Northerner the title of "that incomparable infantry." It also prevented them on occasion from achieving the maximum effect of their heroics. A Confederate charge was likely to be highly erratic in conformation—as "crooked as a ram's horn," said one Southern general—and the men were perfectly capable of substituting their judgments for that of their officers. Both armies were highly individualistic, but the Northern soldiers submitted more readily to discipline. Perhaps the best summary is that the Northerner was a better soldier, the Southerner a better fighting man.

But both armies were splendid fighting aggregations. If they had not possessed a special quality, they could not have endured the appalling casualty rates of the war. The total service deaths were 360,000 for the North and 258,000 for the South. The total of 618,000 is slightly more than the number in all of America's other wars combined. Of the Northern deaths, 110,000 were from battle wounds, and of the Southern, 95,000. Sickness and disease killed more men than bullets did. The total casualty figure becomes more horribly impressive if related to the data of a later and larger war. In World War II the American service deaths were 405,000 out of a population of 135 million. If the World War II ratio of deaths to population had equaled that of the North in the Civil War, the number of fatalities would have reached nearly 2.5 million; if it had equaled the ratio in the South, deaths would have totaled well over five million.

THE generals who led the Civil War armies had, like their men, a common cultural background. Of those who were army commanders, the great majority were graduates of West Point. At the top command level the Civil War was consistently a West Pointers' fight. Of the 60 biggest battles, graduates of the Academy commanded both sides in 55; in the remaining five a graduate commanded one of the two opposing forces.

No general out of civilian life showed the capacity to direct an army of combined arms—infantry, artillery, cavalry—although possibly Nathan Bedford Forrest, the South's hard-riding and hard-fighting cavalry genius, might have proved the exception if he had been given a fuller opportunity. Civilian generals did fill unit commands competently, however, and some of them rose to lead a corps, the largest unit in an army.

Because of West Point preponderance in the high command posts, the military education and the military concepts of the Academy had a determining

Grover Cleveland was a poor lawyer when the war began; while two brothers served, he hired a substitute so he could support his mother. In 1884, running for President, he was attacked as a draft dodger. But his backers had a ready answer: his opponent, James G. Blaine, had hired a substitute too.

John D. Rockefeller, just starting his sensational business career in 1861, also hired a substitute—although not the 20 or 30 he later boasted. John's brother Frank, 16, chalked "18" on his boot soles, told an enlistment officer "I'm over 18" and was accepted. Frank served three years, was twice wounded.

Major General William S. Rose-crans had light hair and loaded his staff with men similarly endowed—"sandy fellows," he called them—because they were "quick and sharp." But he himself was subject to panic. After his defeat at Chickamauga, Lincoln said he acted "like a duck hit on the head."

Don Carlos Buell was a sour and cautious Union general whose reluctance to do battle was notorious. One subordinate compared him to a dancing master addressing the foe thus: "By your leave, my dear sir, we will have a fight; that is, if you are sufficiently fortified. No hurry; take your time."

influence on the way battles were fought and, in fact, on the whole conduct of the war. The professionals of both armies were steeped in an identical philosophy of strategy and war. Essentially it was a philosophy that was 18th Century in origin and outlook. It emphasized victory by maneuver rather than by the decision of battle. It was humane, deprecating the loss of life. It favored the occupation of territory and places above the destruction of enemy armies. It assumed that war was a professional exercise, to be carried on by professionals without much reference to the political objectives of governments. This was the doctrine of generals in the first of the modern wars, and with some the doctrine hardened into dogma and was never shaken off.

In the first stages of the war the influence of traditionalism was more injurious to Northern than to Southern generalship. The offensive was by tradition the most potent weapon in war. Northern generals translated this to mean offensives against places. Able to requisition supplies without limit from an abundant economy, they loaded themselves down with so much useless equipment that it slowed their offensives to a parade. One field army in the Western theater in 1863 had on hand 3,000 wagons, 600 ambulances, 50,000 horses and mules, 24,000 bales of hay and 200,000 bushels of grain, and although much of this was necessary, some of it was excess. "This expanding, and piling up of *impedimenta*," Lincoln told one general, "has been, so far, almost our ruin, and will be our final ruin if it is not abandoned."

Southern generals were more fortunate. Because their government did not look to the acquisition of enemy territory, they could employ the offensive against enemy armies rather than places. Moreover, Southern generals, operating with far skimpier resources, could not afford to wait for a big build-up in men and equipment; they had to act quickly with what they had.

The result was to make Southern generalship appear more dashing, original and modern than Northern. But the advantage was largely superficial. Actually Southern generals, representing a conservative society, were conservative practitioners of war. They were, if anything, even more traditional than their Northern counterparts. The difference was that they practiced their art with brilliance, with a definite style, while the Northern officers for the most part executed theirs without imagination and in some cases without even competence. The distinguishing quality about Southern generalship, however, is that it did not grow. It was good within limits, and it remained good, but always within the same limits. The North, on the other hand, was finally able to bring forward generals who could rise above dogma, who could adopt new ways of war, who were truly modern soldiers.

NORTHERN leadership in the Eastern theater, chiefly the area between Washington and Richmond, was inept almost to the very end. The army commanders there—George B. McClellan, John Pope, Ambrose Burnside, Joseph Hooker, George G. Meade—all lacked the ability to direct large armies to decisive victories. The cocky and magnetic McClellan could train an army expertly, but he could not bring himself to put the fine instrument he created to the decision of battle. He did not have the temperament for field command. Burnside did not have the mentality required of a good general. Pope was willing to fight but was imprudent and a poor handler of troops. Hooker could plan a good battle but lost his nerve at the crucial moment. Meade, the best of the lot, was a competent soldier, but he was afflicted with a defensive psychology and did not have the capacity to finish off an opponent.

The opposing Southern leadership was epitomized by the South's greatest soldier, Robert E. Lee. Fifty-four years of age at the beginning of the war, Lee was a magnificent physical specimen. He was five feet eleven inches in height and weighed about 170 pounds. People who looked at him always thought he was much larger. That was because of his impressive head and shoulders and his majestic bearing. On horseback he seemed to his worshipful soldiers almost like a god. Outwardly simple and open in manner, he was actually a person of much complexity who hid his inner self even from intimates. Always he lived under a rigid discipline and under rigid rules and with a stern devotion to duty. Here was no hell-for-leather cavalier who did whatever his desires indicated, no common Southern type, but a man of immense restraint, a man who kept himself under iron wraps. He was given to uttering maxims, and a favorite one was: "Teach him he must deny himself."

Lee was a superb theater and army commander, a bold strategist, a better than average tactician, and a master of both offensive and defensive war. No general on either side could so arouse the dogged devotion of the common soldier or get so much out of an army. It was his fortune, as commander of the Army of Northern Virginia, to be assisted by some of the ablest subordinate officers of the war, among them two of its best corps leaders, Thomas J. Jackson and James Longstreet. Jackson, who won his sobriquet of "Stonewall" by his stand at the first battle of Bull Run, fought for the Confederacy with a religious fervor. "God blessed our arms with victory today" was a typical Jackson way of starting a battle dispatch. He and Lee seemed to understand instinctively the working of each other's minds, and Lee used Jackson to execute the flanking movements that were "Marse Robert's" favorite strategy. Longstreet, massive and solid, lacked Jackson's daring, but the "Old War Horse," as Lee called him, was a fine handler of troops and a dogged fighter.

IN the vast Western theater, the region between the Appalachian Mountains and the Mississippi River, the situation was reversed. There the Confederate army commanders—Albert Sidney Johnston, P.G.T. Beauregard, Braxton Bragg, Joseph E. Johnston and John B. Hood—were at best no better than adequate, and some of them fell short of the mark. A. S. Johnston, who was killed in battle early in 1862, showed a brilliant promise that was never fulfilled; he failed to act up to the responsibilities of command. Beauregard might have been a good general. But his Gallic effervescence aroused distrust, and he became involved in a feud with President Davis that destroyed his usefulness. Bragg had real strategic ability but lacked the resolution to put his fine plans through to completion. Hood was a bold fighter and a superb corps commander who should never have gone higher. J. E. Johnston, "Uncle Joe" to his devoted troops, was the most puzzling of them all. He gave every indication of greatness and yet did not accomplish a single solid success. He possessed every quality but the vital one—the ability to destroy the enemy.

The general level of Union command in the West—personified at first by men like Henry W. Halleck, Don Carlos Buell and William S. Rosecrans—was no higher. Halleck was a good administrator and desk soldier who had no capacity for field command. Buell was a more colorless McClellan. Rosecrans had a good strategic sense and was a master of maneuver but in a critical situation tended to lose control of himself and of a battle.

Joseph E. Johnston was a jaunty Rebel general who feuded for many years with Jefferson Davis —starting, so the story goes, when both were at West Point. In later years Johnston lost his hair from some illness; in the war he always wore a hat at the table, to the vast amusement of his servants.

The brilliant cavalry commander Nathan Bedford Forrest entered the Confederate army as a private and emerged a lieutenant general four years later. In the process he had 29 horses shot out from under him and was repeatedly wounded. Joseph E. Johnston called him the greatest soldier of the entire war.

The brass Napoleon, an artillery piece developed in France under Emperor Napoleon III, was one of the most effective weapons of the war. In the North it was manufactured by a number of factories, including the Massachusetts copper company founded in 1800 by the Boston patriot, Paul Revere.

Yet it was in the West that the North's great soldiers developed; many went on from there to win in other theaters. George H. Thomas, although inclined to prepare in too much detail before striking, was one of the hardest-hitting of all generals when he finally moved; on defense he was unshakable. Philip Sheridan made a name as a brilliant cavalry leader, and in the last phase of the war proved that he could handle an army of combined arms. William T. Sherman introduced new ways of war, terrible new ways that employed economic and psychological warfare against the civilian population of the enemy.

But the greatest of them all was Ulysses S. Grant, who emerged as the North's best fighting general of any theater and who in 1864 became general in chief of Union forces in all theaters. He and Lee stand together and alone as the supreme military figures of the war. They were battle captains who had the instinct to seek out and destroy the enemy. They had the character to bear up under the lonely responsibility of command. Grant was the better strategist, Lee the abler tactician. Lee was more daring, but Grant understood more fully the nature of modern war. They are, in the last analysis, the only two of the war's generals who deserve to be ranked as great.

NEARLY all the generals of both sides, including the best ones, showed deficiencies in tactics, the arrangement and direction of troops on the battlefield. The typical assault formation of the war, a modification of European practice, was an advance in a succession of lines of two ranks each. The lines, rolling forward like recurring waves, were supposed to shock and eventually to drive the enemy. It hardly ever worked out that way. A frontal attack against a determined foe in a strong position hardly ever succeeded.

There were two reasons for the failure of tactics to achieve the expected result. The line formation had been devised for the relatively open terrain of Europe, where the troops could advance in regular designs and could continue to move under the direct eye of their commander. In the American terrain, cut up with woods, ravines and hills, such an advance was next to impossible. The units became separated from one another, and they moved forward in an uneven arrangement and at an uneven rate of speed. They were thus lost to the sight of their general and dissipated much of the impetus of their thrust.

More important than geography in disrupting an infantry assault was technology. The weapons of a Civil War army gave it such firepower that it could break up an attack before its own line was struck. "Put a man in a hole, and a good battery on a hill behind him," noted a Federal officer, "and he will beat off three times his number, even if he is not a very good soldier."

Although breech-loading and repeating rifles were introduced late in the war, they were not widely used. The basic weapon of the infantry soldier was the Springfield rifled musket, a muzzle-loading, one-shot gun. It could kill at half a mile but was most effective at 250 yards. A veteran soldier could deliver two to three shots a minute. The basic artillery piece was the brass "Napoleon," loaded from the muzzle and firing one shot. Rifled guns were introduced, but in the wooded country where most of the battles were fought the Napoleon was more effective. Firing solid shot or explosive shells, it had a maximum range of a mile. At ranges of 200 yards or so, loaded with canister shot, it had the murderous effect of a huge sawed-off shotgun.

At Gettysburg the attacking Confederates lost in killed and wounded 301 out of every 1,000 men engaged, and the defending Federals 212 of every 1,000.

Gettysburg, the great set battle piece of the war, also illustrates perfectly the effect of the new weapons on tactics. The Confederates delivered two headlong attacks on successive days, attempting in each to advance in the traditional line formation. In Pickett's charge they halted under fire to achieve a straight alignment, while the awed Federals murmured: "My God, they're dressing the line." As the Gray ranks moved forward, they presented a glorious spectacle. But then the guns struck them. A Federal colonel described what happened: "The distinct, graceful lines of the rebels underwent an instantaneous transformation. They were at once enveloped in a dense cloud of dust. Arms, heads, blankets, guns and knapsacks were tossed into the clear air. Their track, as they advanced, was strewn with dead and wounded. A moan went up from the field distinctly to be heard amid the storm of battle." A Confederate artillerist recorded with horror a sight he saw after one attack: "It would have satiated the most bloodthirsty and cruel man on God's earth. There were, in a few feet of us . . . seventy nine (79) North Carolinians laying dead in a straight line. I stood on their right and looked down their line. It was perfectly dressed. Three had fallen to the front, the rest had fallen backward; yet the feet of all these dead men were in a perfectly straight line."

The Civil War generals are often criticized for failing to shift to a more extended formation. Some of them did experiment with new forms—for example, sending their men forward in a succession of rushes without regard to symmetry. But it was not entirely military conservatism that held back change. A constant requirement in battle is control—a commander has to maintain direction of his men at all times. A Civil War general possessed only elementary forms of communication with his troops, such as bugle calls, once they had passed beyond his sight. He had enough difficulty controlling them in a static situation; in a fluid one he would have been helpless. There had been a revolution in weapons, but the revolution in communications that would enable a general to keep in touch with scattered forces was far in the future.

O{\scriptsize N} the highest level of war, the determination of policy, both sides fought for unlimited objectives. The policy of the North was to restore the Union by force. This could not be accomplished by a mere success of arms. The North had to defeat the Confederate armies, but it had also to occupy large and vital Southern areas and to convince the Southern people that their cause was hopeless. The policy of the South was to win its independence by force. The South did not have to accomplish the same kind of total victory that the North did, but its aims were no more capable of being compromised.

Strategy, defined most broadly, is the process employed to secure the aims of policy. By the very nature of Northern policy, the strategy of the North had to be offensive. The framers of Southern strategy, among whom President Jefferson Davis had the determining voice, decided to adopt a defensive strategy, to hold every part of the long Southern border. In part the decision was a forced reaction to Northern strategy, and in part it was a response to political requirements: To abandon any Southern area, even if not defensible or not vital, would depress popular morale. Besides, the South had no ambitions to acquire Northern territory, and a defensive strategy seemed logical.

But the South's real objective was to convince the North that it could not be conquered. Quite possibly this might be accomplished by standing back and waiting for attacks and repelling all of them from all directions. But in

A Civil War bugler sounds a call. Many buglers invented calls, and soldiers sometimes put words to these. One used in Union General Daniel Butterfield's brigade went: "Dan, Dan, Dan, Butterfield!" Another poignant melody used in the same brigade swept the army and became famous. It was "Taps."

Clara Barton, a patent-office worker, heard about a shortage of medical supplies in the Union army and placed an ad in a New England newspaper soliciting help. Supplies poured in, and as a nurse she began a career of public service which culminated in 1881 when she organized the American Red Cross.

the early stages of the war when it was strongest, the South might better have persuaded the Union of its invincibility by invading, by winning victories on Northern soil, not for the purpose of occupation but to demonstrate Southern power. The South did attempt two offensives, a double-pronged one in 1862 into Maryland and Kentucky and in 1863 a thrust into Pennsylvania. Both were turned back, partly because they were not made in sufficient strength; some troops were retained for defense in the South.

MEN could sit at desks and formulate strategic schemes, but everything they devised was influenced and even controlled by impersonal forces, the most compelling of which was geography. The physical features of the South, the scene of most of the battles, determined that the fighting would be done in fairly well-delineated theaters. Because of the Appalachian Mountain barrier, neither government could conduct unified operations in the region between the Atlantic Coast and the Mississippi River. The area east of the mountains was known as the Eastern theater and the area west of them to the Mississippi as the Western theater. Beyond the river, in the states of Louisiana, Arkansas and Texas, was a sub-theater called the Trans-Mississippi.

In the Eastern theater the important operations took place in Virginia, specifically in the region between the rival capitals of Washington and Richmond, separated by a distance of only about 100 marching miles. Here the object of the Federals, on the offensive and hence having the initiative, was to capture Richmond and defeat the defending Confederate army. Usually the invaders headed straight south from Washington toward their goal, although on occasion they moved on the waterways to the east of Richmond. As the contending armies surged back and forth within this constricted space, they sometimes fought twice on the same field. There were two battles of Bull Run, or Manassas (the Federals generally named battles after the closest natural feature, usually a stream, and the Confederates after the nearest human settlement), there were two encounters in the dreary land south of the Rapidan River known as the Wilderness, and two campaigns were fought between the York and James Rivers east of Richmond. Confederate Virginia became literally a place of death.

Affecting all operations in Virginia was a possible secondary route farther to the west, the Shenandoah Valley, universally referred to simply as the Valley. The Valley was an important source of food to the Confederate army, and because of the direction it ran in—from southwest to northeast—it facilitated movements by the Confederates. They were strikingly successful in giving the impression that from its cover they meant to threaten Washington, thus forcing the Federals to detach strength from their main effort against Richmond. Elsewhere in the Eastern theater the Federals stabbed at Confederate railroad communications on the long coastline and tried fruitlessly to take Charleston with naval attacks.

In the Western theater the first objective of Northern strategy was to seize control of the Mississippi River line, thus isolating the Trans-Mississippi Confederacy and dividing the South into two parts. Moving on the river or on streams parallel to it with both land and naval forces, the Federals accomplished their aim by mid-1863. Then they developed a second objective, to grasp the Tennessee River line and its key city, Chattanooga. The town was like a door opening into the inner recesses of the South, and from it the Federals could drive into Georgia or Alabama to divide the South again. The Federals would eventually secure their base, but not until the end of 1863 and after hard fighting.

Neither side was able to commit large resources to the Trans-Mississippi theater, and it remained a backwater of the main conflict. The Federals occupied New Orleans and southern Louisiana and took the northern half of Arkansas. But, although they tried, they could not expand their conquests. After the seizure of the Mississippi line, however, it did not greatly matter what they did west of the river. Merely by holding the river and their present positions, they could contain and neutralize the whole theater.

All of these strategic concepts were worked out after the war began and as it developed. At the start, neither government followed even a general plan of operations. The new Confederate government could hardly have had a plan ready, although one was not beyond the capacities of the United States government. But no agency in the United States military system was charged with the function of studying strategy or preparing possible strategic designs.

At the head of the Northern army organization was the general in chief. Early in 1861 this was 75-year-old Winfield Scott, who could not mount a horse without help. Under him was a group of administrators loosely called the "general staff." They bore no resemblance to the general staffs of later wars. Their work was routine and technical, concerned with the "housekeeping" of the army, and they never met as a group.

The supreme figure in this simple command system was the President, the constitutional commander in chief of all the armed forces. In contrast with the Southern President, the Northern President had had no military education and no significant military experience. Yet Abraham Lincoln proved to be a greater war director than Jefferson Davis. He developed into a fine strategist, better than most of his generals, possibly because his thinking was not bound by the limits of doctrine.

Almost immediately Lincoln realized that enemy armies rather than places were the proper objectives of his armies. Grasping that numbers were on the side of the North, he constantly urged his generals to maintain a steady pressure on the whole circumference of the Confederacy until a weak spot was found and a penetration effected. By modern standards he interfered too much with military matters. But all his interferences were designed to galvanize the war effort, to force his generals to greater offensive endeavors. If he had not interfered as he did, the Union cause might well have failed.

Typical military punishments, employed by both armies, are depicted in these sketches by Charles W. Reed, a veteran of the Union army. "Bucking and gagging" (top) was a penalty for such offenses as straggling or insubordination. Thievery was penalized not only by the use of placards (below), but also by attiring the culprit in a barrel and parading him before the regiment.

Although Lincoln had no hesitation in imposing his will on the generals, he continually sought for ways to improve the command system. When old General Scott retired in November 1861, Lincoln appointed as his successor young George B. McClellan, who also commanded the Federal field army in the East. McClellan had no taste or talent for framing grand strategy, and when he took the field in the spring of 1862, Lincoln relieved him from supreme command. To take his place the President called to Washington Henry W. Halleck. Halleck had been an apparently successful departmental commander in the West—although Grant was really responsible for his victories—and he was known as a soldier-scholar; men called him "Old Brains." He was unimpressive in appearance, with bulging eyes and a shifty demeanor—he had a habit of holding his head sideways, which caused one officer to remark that conversing with him was like talking to somebody over your shoulder—but he seemed to have every technical qualification for the post. He soon demonstrated that he was not up to it. He was full of bookish learning and delighted to give advice, but he dodged the responsibility of making decisions. Again, Lincoln had to take on the burden of acting as general in chief as well as commander in chief, although Halleck stayed as a kind of military adviser.

Then in 1864 came the last and most significant change. U.S. Grant, fresh from a series of shining victories in the West, was named general in chief and charged with the function of over-all strategic planning. Halleck, who was an ideal office soldier, became "chief of staff," a liaison man between Lincoln and Grant, and between Grant and the departmental commanders under him.

GRANT was a curious and puzzling man. A failure in everything he touched before the war, in the war he suddenly became great. People were always looking for visible signs of distinction in Grant. Most of them were disappointed. In appearance he was one of the most unimpressive of Civil War generals—slight in stature, a man of five feet eight inches and 135 pounds, with no magnetism of person or dash of manner. He could have passed, as one perceptive observer wrote, for "a dumpy and slouchy little subaltern." But, this same man noted, Grant was really an extraordinary figure, on whom in a crisis "all around, whether few in number or a great army as here, would instinctively lean."

He had come through many tests on his way up, and he proved equal to the top command post. He was the one soldier of the war who could think realistically about grand strategy, strategy for all theaters and all fronts. Lincoln trusted him and gave him a relatively free hand. But Grant knew what Lincoln wanted in the way of strategy and sensibly made his plans conform to the President's concepts. Grant's master design for 1864 called for the very kind of offensive Lincoln had been advocating almost from the war's beginning—a series of simultaneous advances, a constant and relentless pressure against the entire strategic line of the Confederacy. It was a good plan, and it produced the victories that broke the back of the Confederacy. Lincoln, Grant, Congress and the American people among them had finally devised a modern command system for a modern war.

The Confederacy never lifted its arrangements to such a level. Davis, like Lincoln, exercised a dominating influence in the formulation of strategy. But whereas Lincoln acted to make a sound offensive strategy more offensive, Davis acted to make a questionable defensive strategy more defensive. Early in 1862 Davis assigned Lee, who had not yet made his great field reputation, to command all Confederate armies "under the direction of the President." Lee acted more as a military adviser than a general in chief, and after a few months departed to assume command of the Confederate army in Virginia.

Not until 1864 did Davis appoint another adviser. Then he selected Braxton Bragg, who had failed in field command and who knew better than to present any views Davis might not like. In the closing months of the war Davis, under congressional pressure, again named Lee as general in chief. Lee, burdened with the command of an army and preoccupied with the war in Virginia, did not have the time or the inclination to supervise planning on all fronts, and the Confederacy ended the war with much the same system that it had begun with. The cultures of the two nations influenced their strategic arrange-

"You must throw away that cigar, sir!" a black sentry commands General Ulysses Grant as he passes the commissary storehouse. The story of the willingness of a black soldier to issue an order to a white general, though probably exaggerated, delighted abolitionists. Some 185,000 black soldiers served in the Union forces; about 100 of them were commissioned officers.

ments as surely as every other aspect of their warmaking. For the progressive and centralized North it was comparatively easy to build a modern command system. For the static and decentralized South it proved impossible.

As the combatant powers approached the ordeal of battle, all the great material factors pointed to a Northern victory. The North had a larger population, over 22 million to the South's nine million. Both figures require some qualification. Included in the Northern total are the four loyal slave states of Missouri, Kentucky, Delaware and Maryland, which contained thousands of Southern supporters, and the Pacific Coast states, which took no direct part in the war. A fair estimate of the "military" population of the North would be 20 million. Included in the Southern total are the Negro slaves; without them the South's military, or white, population was between five and six million. But although the slaves were not used for army service, they were still a military asset; by their presence as laborers they freed a certain number of white men for service.

No matter how the odds are calculated—and 3 to 1 would seem reasonably accurate—the North had a manpower advantage. It was not, however, as decisive as it seems. Operating on the offensive, the North needed more men to guard its supply lines and to garrison key points in a hostile country. More important, the South brought its manpower into the field more quickly than the North. In the first half of the war the size of the contending armies on many a field was not greatly different and certainly not decisive. It was not beyond possibility that up to 1863 the South might have achieved independence by a military victory.

More significant than the manpower advantage was the North's economic superiority, and this factor became more apparent as time passed. The North had 75 per cent of the total wealth produced in the country, 67 per cent of the farms, 81 per cent of the factories and 66 per cent of the railroad mileage. Moreover, the North had the capacity to produce new wealth during the war, while the South lived off and consumed its accumulated wealth.

The North possessed finally the great weapon of sea power. The Union navy grew during the war from a small force of 90 ships and 9,000 sailors to a formidable fleet of 670 ships and 51,000 men. The Confederate navy counted scarcely more than 130 ships and 4,000 men. In two vital ways the Union navy served the war effort. It established a blockade of the long Southern coast, and although the blockade was never completely effective, it was a damaging form of economic warfare. And in the Western theater the navy co-operated as an equal with the army in reducing the vast stretches of that region.

THE brutal facts of arithmetic seemed to doom the Southern cause from the start. Perhaps it was always a doomed cause. Yet the South fought on for four years, and at times even people in the North seemed willing to concede that it might win. Indeed, one of the South's best opportunities to win independence lay in what might be called the psychology of the war. Southerners were fighting for something very definite, very easy to fight for. They merely wanted to be let alone. The North's goals, nationalism and emancipation, were abstract and harder to fight for; moreover, if the North quit the war it would still enjoy its independence. All the South had to do was to convince the North it could not be conquered. On the eve of battle, nobody dreamed the result was foreordained—least of all the men who would do the fighting.

Advancing in battle in the Peninsular Campaign, Union soldiers display the crisp formation that caused thousands of fighting men to be mowed down by small arms and artillery fire early in the war. Officers of all ranks customarily marched or rode at the head of their troops; by the war's end only seven of 47 major generals who fought for Lee were still in service.

19

"OUR SPECIAL ARTIST" is the caption of this Winslow Homer picture from *Harper's Weekly* of June 14, 1862. It shows a combat artist—probably Homer—sketching two giants of the 1st Maine Regiment. Artists usually made hasty drawings which were then engraved—with added details—by their journals.

A perceptive artist at the front

THE Civil War was the first American conflict involving citizen-soldiers on a large scale. One American in 12 saw service, either Union or Confederate, and virtually every family had someone out at the front. Among the folks back home, therefore, an unprecedented demand arose for news—not only of victories or defeats but of how their menfolk were doing. To satisfy this appetite, a new species of journalist came into prominence—the special artist. He worked for an illustrated weekly newspaper and his assignment was to go wherever the winds of combat blew and to sketch what he saw, be it battle, boredom or bravado. There were about 30 such special artists and after the war most of them slipped into obscurity.

The one notable exception was Winslow Homer, who was to be one of America's greatest artists. Even in 1861, when he was an unknown young illustrator covering the Army of the Potomac, his work had a unique vitality. Other artists drew busy but oddly synthetic battle panoramas, with handsome soldiers in neat uniform. Homer's combat scenes have the smell of gunpowder and the shriek of death under a trampling horse. Moreover, as every soldier knows, war is partly fighting, partly waiting—and Homer's pictures preserve an unmatched record of the Civil War's citizen-soldier in his unguarded moments, between battles, in the camp, on the move and in the trenches.

"TWO FEDERAL SCOUTS," businesslike in their Confederate uniforms, prepare to slip into enemy territory. The scouts of those days usually operated behind the lines.

Bivouac boredom in the days of the Blue and the Gray

As Winslow Homer portrayed it, the Civil War, like most wars, was composed 10 per cent of battles and 90 per cent of boredom. The grinding monotony of picket duty was merely a break in the even greater monotony of camp life. Even soldiers facing the enemy in the long build-up before a battle often found time hanging heavy. At such times the only ones who did much fighting were the members of an occasional patrol and the ubiquitous snipers, who were a constant hazard to both sides in an era when many a farm boy was able to hit a squirrel in the eye at 100 yards.

Sometimes the patrols would enliven things in camp by bringing back a bag of prisoners. Sometimes there would be a review or perhaps a laborious shifting of a campsite to a better spot a few miles away. But mostly there was waiting. For some men any kind of excitement was preferable to doing nothing, and they often took foolhardy chances to stir things up *(lower right)*.

"A SHARPSHOOTER ON PICKET DUTY" sights along his rifle from a perch in a tree, watching for enemy movement. Sharpshooters were picked men, usually armed with excellent rifles.

"In Front of Yorktown," waiting for the month-long siege of 1862 to end, bored, hungry, homesick Federal soldiers gather around a campfire.

"DARING THE ENEMY" in a senseless challenge prompted by a combination of bravado and frustration, an infantryman shouts defiance at Confederates from atop Union battlements.

"PRISONERS FROM THE FRONT," three ragged rebels stand in attitudes of affected casualness, apprehension and studied defiance before a young, well-groomed officer of the Union army. This canvas, which was first exhibited in the spring of 1866, created a sensation and launched Homer as a serious painter.

The horrors of fierce combat and primitive medicine

THE Civil War was the most terrible that Americans have ever fought. The casualties were appalling—nearly one out of every four men in service died of disease, wounds or other causes. During much of the war 18th Century tactics contended against modern weapons, and often in dense woodland. The result was unparalleled horror. Infantrymen often advanced shoulder to shoulder, Napoleonic-style, into a butchering fire from accurate new rifled muskets, or found themselves pinned down in a wild tangle by an invisible foe.

For the soldiers of both North and South the horror of combat was compounded by the knowledge that there was no such thing as a simple wound. In an era of primitive medicine every battle injury had to be considered serious—fatal at worst, often maiming at best.

"FROM RICHMOND": two soldiers returning from the front display wounds they received in the fighting around the Rebel capital. Almost 50 per cent of all the Civil War wounded died.

"A SKIRMISH IN THE WILDERNESS" pits a squad of Northerners against an unseen enemy. Homer's canvas at first appears to be simply a forest scene, and thus magnificently conveys the atmosphere of dense woods in which this fierce encounter was fought near Fredericksburg, Virginia, in May 1864. In two days at the Wilderness the Union lost 18,000 dead and wounded.

Housekeeping problems for men in the camps

ALTHOUGH commanders on both sides tried to impose some order on armies in bivouac, it was usually a losing fight. Neat tent rows soon fell prey to soldier idiosyncrasies. Some men slept on the ground under canvas shelter halves. Others built log walls and used the canvas for a roof. Conical Sibley tents held 12 soldiers sleeping closely packed with their feet toward the center. And when an army really settled in for a long stay, soldiers built luxurious log huts, each boasting a fireplace with a barrel chimney.

In these encampments soldiers played, wrote letters and tried to improve their food—if they had a chance amid their numerous duties. Reveille ushered in a day which might include eight hours of drilling, five roll calls and a dress parade. Soldiers and generals alike were trying to cope with the same problem: troops not engaged in killing the enemy had to find a way of killing time.

"REVEILLE," played by a bugler and two drummers, finds a few soldiers already awake around a fire while others come streaming from their tents for morning roll call.

"PITCHING HORSESHOES" depicts gaudy soldiers at a listless game. The canopy of boughs served as a protection from the hot sun—soldiers wore wool all year long.

"HOME SWEET HOME" is the ironic title of this painting. Besides the shelter halves in the foreground Homer's picture shows distant log-walled dwellings and a Sibley tent.

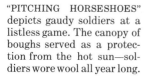

"LAST GOOSE AT YORKTOWN" is the quarry of two hungry Federal soldiers. Barrel chimneys like that on the log hut often caught fire—much to the merriment of the neighbors.

27

The swift, hazardous route from rookie to veteran

IN this war of civilians, the transition from shapeless recruit *(opposite page)* to hard-bitten veteran *(below)* was often a rapid one. In most cases the process depended less on training than it did on experience. The new soldier learned by sleeping on the ground, by going hungry, by scrounging for firewood among a farmer's fence posts, and most of all by smelling gunpowder. Once a man had been under fire (or had "seen the elephant," in the idiom of the time) he lost the fresh-faced naiveté of the recruit—and along with it much of his former belief in his own invincibility. What he did not learn from battle he picked up from his colleagues in arms—not only how to do his work properly, but how to escape it entirely *(right)*. In the end, by some mysterious process, whether he was a Yank or a Reb he emerged, as one general said of his own men, a soldier of "invincible fighting courage and stamina, worthy of a great . . . nation."

"PLAYING OLD SOLDIER," Civil War terminology for gold-bricking, a soldier sticks out his tongue for the doctor. Real sickness was all too common; 220,000 men died of disease in the Union army alone.

"YOUNG UNIONIST," or a "fresh fish" as oldtimers called them, stands uncomfortably in an overcoat several sizes too big. At least 10,000 boys from 13 to 17 saw service; one went into battle at age nine.

"RAINY DAY IN CAMP" finds five cavalrymen warming themselves at a cooking fire. The men often prepared their own food —usually about a pound of salt pork plus some hardtack, boiled to kill the weevils.

2. "FORWARD TO RICHMOND"

EVERYBODY in the North—the newspapers, the politicians and the public —seemed to be shouting "Forward to Richmond" in that summer of 1861 when the war was just getting under way. People had the vaguest notions as to what constituted a proper military objective for Northern forces to strike at; they knew only that they wanted something struck. "We want the army to kill somebody," one citizen later explained to his senator. Then the news came that the Confederate Congress planned to convene in Richmond on July 20. The North exploded in anger. Here at last was an objective for the army that was gathering around Washington: Richmond, the Rebel capital and seat of treason.

In the last week in June the New York *Tribune* began urging in every edition: "Forward to Richmond! Forward to Richmond! The Rebel Congress must not be allowed to meet there on the 20th of July! By that date the place must be held by the National Army!" The "Nation's War Cry," the *Tribune* called its daily demand, and suddenly it was taken up all over the North. Such a magnificent stroke, it was felt, would end the war at once.

In the White House Lincoln listened to the popular clamor. He was not impressed with the symbolic importance of breaking up the Confederate Congress. But at this stage he had his share of the national innocence about war. He too thought it would be a short war, and in the military situation he saw an opportunity to exploit the North's pulsing enthusiasm for a forward

A WINTER SENTRY guards a Rebel encampment early in the war, when Southern hopes were strong and Southern forces still well fed, warmly clothed and high in spirit.

movement and at the same time to accomplish a perhaps decisive result.

Near Washington was the principal Federal army, more than 30,000 men under Irvin McDowell, a regular officer just jumped up from major to brigadier general. At the northern end of the Shenandoah Valley, 50 miles away, was an array of 14,000 troops commanded by General Robert Patterson, a venerable militia soldier whose experience went back to the War of 1812. Confronting the Federals was an army of more than 20,000 men around Manassas, about 30 miles southwest of Washington, commanded by General P.G.T. Beauregard, the recent hero of Fort Sumter. In the Valley there was an aggregation of 10,000 under General Joseph E. Johnston.

In all, some 45,000 Federals faced 30,000 Confederates. As Lincoln saw it, there was in this arrangement of numbers the chance for a smashing blow: if McDowell with his superior army could advance and knock out Beauregard's army, the war might end right there. McDowell was ordered to move. The Union general objected to an immediate offensive on the ground that his troops were green, but his argument fell on deaf ears. As McDowell said later, the answer he kept getting, presumably from Lincoln, was: "You are green . . . but they are green also . . ." The one clear fact was that the numbers gave the odds to the Federals. McDowell was assured that if Johnston, in the Valley, tried to go to Beauregard's aid, Patterson would follow and hold him.

Although he was not entirely satisfied, McDowell made plans for an advance in mid-July. He was a tall and heavy man, given to awesome feats of eating, such as gulping down a whole watermelon for dessert, but he was an unlucky general. Nearly always he made good plans which for some reason went awry. The plan that he designed now was sound enough and it might have succeeded in defeating Beauregard's army—if it had worked.

McDowell moved his forces out on July 16. Beauregard responded by concentrating his own forces behind Bull Run, a small stream north of Manassas. The dashing and dapper Creole was a good handler of troops in the field, but before a battle he was likely to oscillate between extremes of pessimism and optimism. Now, even before contact with McDowell had been made, Beauregard excitedly called on the government to order Johnston to join him. President Davis wisely refused to move the Valley force until McDowell's intentions were more fully developed. If Johnston moved too soon to meet Beauregard, Patterson would move to join McDowell, and the odds would tip still more in favor of the Federals. Not until McDowell began to maneuver north of Bull Run did the government order Johnston to Manassas. Making the journey by rail, most of the Valley army reached Beauregard the day before battle was joined. It was a daring gamble and it worked. In the first big encounter of the war, the Battle of Bull Run, the contending forces would be approximately equal in size—some 30,000 each.

BOTH commanders decided to take the offensive. Although Johnston was the ranking Southern general on the field, he permitted Beauregard, who knew the ground better, to plan the battle. The rival commanders devised movements that were fairly complex, and curiously, both fixed upon identical strategies. McDowell, masking his intentions with demonstrations on his front, would send a column up Bull Run to cross and come down and turn the Confederate left. Beauregard, massing his strength on his right, would strike across the run and turn the Federal left. The Creole, all optimism now

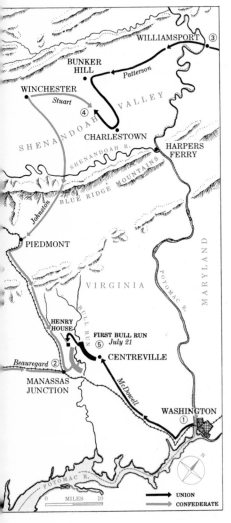

BULL RUN:

THE REBELS SCORE

On July 16, 1861, General Irvin McDowell moved from Washington (1) to attack General P.G.T. Beauregard's Confederates near Manassas Junction (2). General Robert Patterson, 65 miles away at Williamsport (3), was ordered to contain General Joseph E. Johnston's Rebel troops in the Shenandoah Valley. But a feint by Jeb Stuart's cavalry (4) confused Patterson, and Johnston slipped south by railroad to join Beauregard. At Bull Run (5) both armies launched attacks on their right, but at Henry House, Federal troops panicked— and fled 30 miles to Washington.

that he was reinforced, was gaily confident that he could crush the invaders.

Beauregard was still exuberant when the battle began at about five on the morning of July 21. He and Johnston rode to a position midway on the Confederate line and waited for the attack on the right to jump off. Nothing happened, and soon Beauregard learned that there was some kind of Federal action developing on his own left. Deciding that the report portended no more than an enemy demonstration, Beauregard shifted some units to his left and made some adjustments on his right, where he still expected to deliver his main stroke. But still nothing happened. Unknown to Beauregard, his orders had not been delivered to all the officers on the right, and the situation in this sector was hopelessly snarled. Meanwhile the noise of battle on the left swelled in volume. Johnston could stand it no longer. "The battle is there," he cried, "I am going," and spurred off. Beauregard, at last concerned, ordered all available units moved to the left, and followed.

The two generals found a potentially disastrous situation. The Federal flanking movement had ground forward against relatively light Confederate resistance until it came to a temporary halt at an eminence called the Henry House Hill. The defending Gray line had been bent back from Bull Run and faced almost directly west. Desperately both Beauregard and McDowell began to pile in more men, trying to gain the ascendancy.

General Pierre G. T. Beauregard, dashing hero of First Bull Run (or First Manassas, as it was known in the Confederacy), was one of the South's heroes early in the war and the subject of many songs and poems. One written after the Bull Run victory combined praise for the general with a dig at the routed Yankees. It was called "The Beauregard Manassas Quick-step."

IN this feverish race the Confederates won. A new Federal thrust moved ahead—and then faltered. Beauregard, realizing the crucial moment had come, ordered a counterattack. The Gray units surged forward, and then it happened—what inevitably had to happen to one of these armies of green, untrained boys after hours of fighting on a hot July day. Any sudden turn of events might have caused either side to panic, and the Confederate advance did it to the Federals. If the Rebels could attack, ran the thinking in the Blue ranks, then they must have been reinforced and they must be irresistible—and let's get out of here, fast! The Federals broke. The withdrawal became a rout. North of the stream the demoralization spread, and McDowell had to retreat all the way to the Washington defenses. It was not an army that streamed back but a mass of fugitives. Hundreds of Northern sightseers who had driven down in buggies to see the fun now fled in panic, clogging the roads. One congressman was captured by Rebel soldiers.

But the Confederates were almost as disorganized by victory as the Federals were by defeat. They made little effort to push a pursuit. Later, Southern critics would charge that a golden opportunity was let slip, that the Confederates could have pressed on and taken Washington itself. This was wishful theorizing. The Confederate army did not have the organization or the equipment to seize the Northern capital. At the moment, the result of the battle seemed welcome enough to most Southerners. Crowed one editor: "The battle of Manassas determines the fate of the war and secures our independence. . . . The war is virtually ended, for the Federal Government can get neither men nor money to prosecute it further, except spasmodically."

The high Southern hopes could not have been more wrong. Bull Run shocked the North but did not blunt its determination to fight on. The government called for more troops and the people braced themselves for what most now realized would be a hard war.

The Federal navy made its weight felt early. Operating from island bases off the Atlantic coast, its vessels patrolled all Southern harbors in an attempt to shut off the South's foreign trade. As the operations of 1862 got under way, the navy played an increasingly important role. Besides making its coastal blockade more and more effective, it acted as a support to the land forces on the rivers of the Western theater. In the process it made use of innovations that were bringing about a revolution in naval warfare. Steam power gradually supplanted sail power, and rifled guns firing explosive shells heralded the end of the age of wooden ships.

CONFEDERATE naval leaders were as keenly aware of the latest trends in water warfare as were those of the North. The Confederates were, in fact, quicker to take advantage of at least one of these changes: the South had to attain immediate superiority, and it could do this only by bringing forth a new naval weapon. Accordingly, Secretary of the Navy Mallory approved plans to fabricate an ironclad ship. Secretary Welles was also pushing the case for ironclads in the North, but he encountered resistance among naval conservatives, and the Confederates got a jump on the North in this respect.

The South fashioned its first ironclad by heroic efforts. When Virginia seceded, the departing Federal authorities had attempted to destroy everything useful in the Norfolk navy yard, among other acts scuttling the frigate *Merrimack*. The Confederates raised her and with the most painful efforts plated her sides with iron. They renamed her the *Virginia*, but in naval history her original title has stuck. She was slow, unwieldy and unreliable—but she was dangerous to any wooden opponent, as she quickly demonstrated.

On March 8, 1862, the new *Merrimack* steamed out of Norfolk harbor to attack the blockading squadron of wooden ships in Hampton Roads. The Federal vessels that stood forward to meet her had almost no chance. Their solid shot rattled off her plating, and her incendiary shells burned through their spars and sides. The *Merrimack* sent one ship to the bottom with her iron ram and destroyed another with her shells. At the end of a bleak day for the United States Navy, the metal monster returned with slow majesty to an anchorage near Norfolk. Consternation reigned in the North.

But the Federal navy had been rushing an ironclad of its own to completion and this vessel, the *Monitor*, was on the way to Hampton Roads. The next scene might have been arranged by the foresight of a master script writer: when the *Merrimack* came out the next day, the *Monitor* was there to meet her. For the first time in naval history two ironclads were to engage in battle.

The antagonists presented striking physical contrasts. The *Merrimack* was high, hulking and clumsy. The *Monitor* was low, almost flat in the water, and maneuverable, and she fired from a revolving turret amidships. Observers likened her to a cheese box on a raft or a tin can on a shingle. The ships fought for over three hours, often at close quarters, but neither possessed the fire power to penetrate the other's armor. Nor could the *Merrimack* ram her nimbler foe. Both finally broke off action by common consent.

In the narrowest tactical sense the result was a standoff. And even if the *Merrimack* had sunk the *Monitor*, it is doubtful if the victory would have meant much. The Confederate ship had so many technical defects that she could not have ventured into ocean waters to challenge the blockade effectively. And in any event the North, with superior resources, could have built enough ironclads to retain naval ascendancy.

The Army Medal of Honor was established in 1862 as an award for gallantry. But in 1863 all the soldiers in one Maine regiment were offered the medal as a bribe when their enlistments expired. Only 309 of them took the bait and stayed to fight, but the remaining 555 received it anyway. In 1917 all 864 medals were withdrawn by Congress as illegal.

In the Western theater the network of waterways favored amphibious operations, and from the beginning the North took advantage of its naval strength in this area. Seizure of the Mississippi line was an early and basic item of Union strategy. To attain their objective, the Federals moved on the Mississippi itself or on streams parallel to it, flanking the Confederates out of their position along the great river.

In 1862 Federal land forces in the West were grouped in two department commands. Based at Louisville was an army of 50,000 men under General Don Carlos Buell. The second command, under Henry W. Halleck, had its headquarters in St. Louis and covered the region west of the Mississippi plus a small corner of Kentucky. Two generals operated under Halleck's direction: Ulysses S. Grant with 20,000 men in western Kentucky and Samuel Curtis with 30,000 in Missouri. That border state had been held for the North through a series of actions directed largely by General Nathaniel Lyon, who had lost his life in the process.

All Confederate forces in the West were under the command of General Albert Sidney Johnston. In Arkansas a detached wing of 20,000 under Earl Van Dorn operated under the loosest supervision from Johnston. In Kentucky the Confederate line ran from Bowling Green on the right, where Johnston had his headquarters, to Columbus on the Mississippi. Its 150-mile length was thinly held by 50,000 men and was badly flawed in the center, where Forts Henry and Donelson commanded the Tennessee and Cumberland rivers flowing north to the Ohio. The forts had been built when Kentucky was asserting an impossible neutrality, and respecting this status, the Confederates had constructed them just over the Tennessee line. As a result, the Confederate center was thrown back from the flanks. Resting on accessible waterways, the forts were an inviting target to a foe with sea power. If they should fall, the two flanks would be isolated and the whole line would be in danger of collapse.

At an exhibition in New Jersey (above), a member of a New Hampshire company of sharpshooters proves his skill. With the bulky telescopic rifle he riddles the "Jeff Davis" target (below). As the unit marched to war, the New York "Tribune" predicted: "If they don't give a good account of themselves, we shall ... have no faith in strong arms ... or 40-pound rifles."

The Northern general who grasped the possibilities was Grant. He was at this stage relatively unknown, but he had already showed that capacity of a great general to strike at the vitals of the enemy. In February, after wringing permission from Halleck, he prepared to attack Fort Henry. The army moved south on the Tennessee, accompanied by a flotilla of ironclad gunboats constructed especially for river service and commanded by crusty Andrew H. Foote, who had faith in both his vessels and Grant. As it turned out, the navy did the job at Henry practically by itself. Its bombardment of the low-lying fort forced the Confederates to surrender after a short resistance.

THEN Grant, demonstrating another quality of great generalship—to keep the momentum of a successful movement going—decided to strike immediately at Donelson. His army marched the 12 miles to the other fort while his naval support moved to the Cumberland. Grant expected another easy victory, but Donelson proved a very different nut to crack. When the Union ships steamed confidently up to deliver their fire, the fort's guns replied with such deadly accuracy that the flotilla, some of its vessels badly damaged, had to retire from the fight. Undaunted, Grant brought troops forward to invest the fort.

Unknown to the Northern general, a curious command situation in the fort was working to his advantage. The ranking Confederate officer was General John B. Floyd, recently Buchanan's Secretary of War. Floyd was convinced

GENERAL JOHN B. FLOYD

GENERAL GIDEON J. PILLOW

GENERAL SIMON B. BUCKNER

These officers joined in a famous game of military musical chairs. Floyd, forced to surrender Fort Donelson to U. S. Grant, handed the onerous chore to Pillow, who hastily passed it to Buckner. As the two others fled, Buckner surrendered to his old friend. After the war the two men resumed their friendship; in 1885 Buckner was a pallbearer at Grant's funeral.

that the fort would have to surrender but he thought that if he surrendered with it, the Federal government might try him for treason—he had been charged with stealing public funds, and also accused of using his Cabinet position to transfer arms to Southern states. So he turned the command over to the second-ranking officer, Gideon Pillow. Pillow, a Tennessee politician, had no intention of being the first Confederate general captured; when Floyd left, Pillow left with him. The command fell to Simon Bolivar Buckner, a courtly Kentuckian who a few years before had helped Grant financially when the latter was temporarily down-and-out.

Manfully Buckner accepted the responsibility. He proposed to Grant an armistice and negotiations. Back came an answer almost brutal in its brevity: "No terms except an unconditional and immediate surrender can be accepted. I propose to move immediately upon your works." Buckner was shocked—he said Grant was "unchivalric"—but he had no choice. He surrendered Donelson on the 16th. More than a battle passed into history that day. A way of war—Buckner's way, the way of knightly men who fought for limited objectives—was going out and a new way, the way of men who cared everything for results and nothing for form, was taking over.

Grant's sledge-hammer blows seemed to throw Albert Sidney Johnston into a daze. Johnston was a handsome and impressive man who was widely regarded as a great general. But in this campaign and its aftermath he did not show the qualities of a departmental commander. After the fall of Henry he decided to pull his flanks back. His decision was sound enough, but at the same time he sent reinforcements into the trap at Donelson. Apparently he thought the garrison could delay Grant and then escape. The result was that Grant secured not only the fort, but also a bag of 15,000 prisoners.

The two Confederate wings fell back and were eventually united at Corinth in northeast Mississippi, not far from the big bend of the Tennessee River. Here the army was safe for the moment, and Johnston and Beauregard—who had come west to act as Johnston's second-in-command—acted energetically to increase its strength. But in the campaign just closed the Confederate cause had suffered a staggering reverse. The South had lost its line in Kentucky and half of Tennessee and part of its hold on the Mississippi. And west of the Mississippi Curtis defeated Van Dorn at Pea Ridge in Arkansas and began the occupation of that state. Many battles in the Civil War can be classified as decisive. But surely in any listing the capture of Henry and Donelson should hold a high place.

D URING the Henry and Donelson campaign "Old Brains" Halleck had sat fussily at his headquarters desk in St. Louis. He had not understood everything Grant was doing, but he had supported his impetuous general. Now he claimed the reward of Grant's victories—the combined Western command, including Buell's army—and the government obliged him. Halleck directed Grant with about 40,000 men to move south up the Tennessee River, and Buell, who had occupied Nashville, to join Grant. His limited concept of war was revealed in his orders, which were merely to break up Confederate railroad communications. Grant debarked his army on the west bank of the Tennessee at Pittsburg Landing, about 30 miles from Corinth. His camps lay between two creeks flowing to the Tennessee; in the center of the area was a little log church called Shiloh. Grant was overly confident; he had whipped the enemy and when Halleck let him loose he would whip them some more. His lines were open, his security precautions elementary.

At Corinth Johnston and Beauregard studied the situation and came to an obvious decision: they must try to deliver a surprise attack on Grant and destroy him before Buell arrived. With 40,000 men, they prepared to move out on April 3 and attack on the 4th. But there now began for the Confederates a costly and frustrating miscarriage of orders and intentions. The march against Grant did not start when it was supposed to—and when it finally did jump off, it was plagued by delays and conducted with too much noise. The men relieved their sense of excitement by whooping and yelling, and many of them, fearing that the damp weather had damaged their guns, tested the weapons by firing them. The attack date was pushed up to the 5th, but on that day Johnston could not get the army deployed in line of battle. As a result of the mix-ups on the march, some units were out of place or missing; by the time the confusion was cleared up it was too late to attack. Beauregard was horrified; certainly the surprise had been lost by now. At a dramatic roadside conference of the top generals, he urged Johnston to call off the attack, but Johnston was resolved. Although he had his faults, lack of courage was not one of them. "Gentlemen, we shall attack at daylight tomorrow," he said calmly. Then he added: "I would fight them if they were a million."

U. S. Grant's real name was Hiram Ulysses, but he was enrolled at West Point by error as Ulysses Simpson and decided to keep the name. After he refused to discuss terms for the surrender of Fort Donelson, people said the U. S. meant "Unconditional Surrender." The victory made him a national idol; well-wishers sent him so many cigars that he gave up his pipe.

By every rule of logic Beauregard should have been right. Yet the Federal high command was unaware even now of the danger. The Union camps lay open and vulnerable on the rolling and forested plateau between the creeks.

As the Confederates moved into line on the morning of the 6th, a Sunday, the sun suddenly broke through the morning mist, and the soldiers excitedly passed the word that it was a good omen. Johnston mounted his horse and said to his staff: "Tonight we will water our horses in the Tennessee River."

The Gray lines rushed forward with a shout, toward the Federal outposts, toward the unsuspecting camps, toward Shiloh church.

In the first impetus of the attack the Confederates drove through the forward line and the camps of the Federals. But soon the advance began to slow. The Gray lines lost their formation in the rugged terrain, and hundreds of hungry Rebels stopped to plunder the stores in the camps. More important, the Federal corps commanders, after the initial shock, rallied their men and improvised a line of defense. Grant arrived on the field after the fighting started, and although shaken he ordered that the troops hold at all cost.

The Confederate advance still ground on, but now slowly and irregularly. Gradually the battle was breaking into many small battles that were fought all over the field under unit commanders. Bullets laced the air. "I imagined," related one Confederate colonel, "if I held up a bushel basket it would fill in a minute." As thick as the bullets was the confusion. A wounded Ohio private was sent to the rear. Soon he was back saying: "Captain, give me a gun. This damned fight ain't got any rear."

As the Federal left retired, some of its units came to a country road sunk a little below the surface of the land around it by much travel. Into this natural trench the Bluecoats piled and made a stand. The Confederate attack surged against it for hours. Eleven times the Southerners charged and each time fell back with bloody losses. With grim aptness they christened the sunken road the "Hornet's Nest." In the meantime the advance on the Confederate

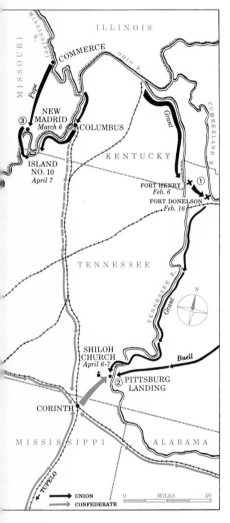

THE WAR IN THE WEST:
CLEARING THE RIVERS

In early 1862 a force under U. S. Grant captured Forts Henry and Donelson (1), opening the Tennessee and Cumberland Rivers. Then Grant was ordered to Pittsburg Landing (2) to threaten Rebel communications. There he was caught napping by Southern troops who had converged on Corinth. Grant, badly mauled in the battle of Shiloh, was saved by the arrival of Buell, and the Confederates were thrown back to Corinth; they ultimately retreated to Tupelo. At the same time Pope, who had taken New Madrid (3) in March, conquered Island No. 10.

left had pushed ahead and was past Shiloh church. The Confederate battle plan was off schedule. It had been to turn the Federals back on a creek to the north and to destroy them there. Instead the attackers were shoving the Union forces eastward toward the Tennessee, where their gunboats lay and where they might join up with Buell.

Johnston saw the fatal drift of events and hurried to his right to spur the lagging attack there. He directed one successful charge and sat observing the retiring enemy. Suddenly he reeled in the saddle. An aide caught him and lifted him to the ground. A stray bullet had severed the artery in his right leg, and in a few minutes he bled to death. Beauregard took over the command and ordered the attack pressed forward. At 5:30 the Southerners finally took the sunken road, after throwing in their last reserves. The Federals then retired toward the Tennessee and threw up a strong line at Pittsburg Landing. After 13 hours of offensive action the Confederates were exhausted, and Beauregard decided to put off the final attack until morning.

Unknown to Beauregard, most of Buell's troops had arrived on the other side of the river. That night 17,000 of them crossed to join Grant, and the Federal commander promptly resolved to seize the initiative. On the morning of the 7th he ordered his men forward. Reversing the pattern of the previous day, he surprised the Confederates. With reinforcements Grant's army again numbered 40,000. But Beauregard, because of his losses and heavy straggling, could put only something more than 20,000 men in line. Slowly the Blue attack crunched forward. Soon Beauregard sensed that if he stood his ground his army would be pounded to pieces. He ordered a withdrawal and retired to Corinth. The battered Federals made no attempt to pursue. Both armies had suffered terrible casualties: over 10,000 men in each killed and wounded, or 25 per cent of their totals. Shiloh was the first bloody battle of the war.

IN the North hard things were said about Grant's being caught by surprise, and temporarily a shadow was cast on his rising star. He had, however, shown real nerve under stress, and he could convincingly claim the victory. The Confederates had failed in their bid to break up the Union concentration, and with nothing to show for their losses were back at Corinth.

That town now became the focal point of the Federal offensive in the West. General Halleck, bringing reinforcements that raised the army strength to 90,000, arrived to command the advance. Moving his host forward ponderously, he took most of May to get into position to attack. Then he elected the slow but sure methods of a siege. Beauregard thereupon decided to evacuate by rail and retire 50 miles southward to Tupelo. Fearing, however, that Halleck might attack him during the withdrawal, Beauregard perpetrated one of the great hoaxes of the war. The night he pulled out he ran an empty train back and forth through the town. Whenever it stopped, soldiers were ordered to shout that more reinforcements were coming. Listening to all the commotion, Halleck prepared for an attack. Country soldiers in Halleck's command laid their ears against the rails, as they were used to doing in their hometowns, and quickly reported to their officers that there was no indication reinforcements were joining Beauregard; on the contrary, trains were going out of Corinth loaded and returning empty. The Federal command paid no attention. Not until they saw smoke rising from burning supplies did they realize they had been duped.

Beauregard had executed a correct move and had done it smartly. But people were criticizing him for allegedly throwing away Johnston's victory at Shiloh. Davis believed the accusation, and was angered at the loss of Corinth. Soon the President found occasion to replace Beauregard with one of the army's corps commanders, Braxton Bragg.

As for Halleck, he and his army might look slightly foolish, but they had captured Corinth, an important railroad center. All along the Mississippi line the Federal tide was flowing forward. Island No. 10 fell to Federal attackers a few hours after Shiloh, and then the Confederate base at Fort Pillow was evacuated. By early June the Federals had moved all the way down to Memphis and had occupied that city.

THEY were also coming up the Mississippi from the south. The seizure of New Orleans was almost from the first a prime objective of Northern strategy. The Northern high command assigned the navy the task of taking the city. Command of the expedition went to Captain David G. Farragut, a 60-year-old Tennessee-born officer, leathery of face and salty in manner. He led into the Gulf of Mexico the most formidable fleet yet assembled in American naval history: 46 craft carrying 286 guns. Heading the armada were four big wooden sloops, one of them his flagship the *Hartford.* Farragut also had some ironclad gunboats with him, but he had doubts about them. "When a shell makes its way into one of those damn teakettles," he snorted, "it can't get out again. It sputters around inside doing all kinds of mischief."

In April the fleet attacked Forts Jackson and St. Philip, the only Confederate defensive points on the lower river. Mortar boats bombarded the works for five days with no effect. The impatient Farragut issued orders to run by the forts. In a blazing battle he forced his way through, destroying a smaller Confederate flotilla as he went. Once above the forts, he met no resistance. New Orleans itself was defenseless. George W. Cable, later destined to be one of America's finest writers but then a boy of 17, recalled the vessels' arrival. "Ah, me! I see them now as they come slowly round Slaughterhouse Point into full view, silent, grim, and terrible; black with men, heavy with deadly portent; the long-banished Stars and Stripes flying against the frowning sky. . . . The crowds on the levee howled and screamed with rage. The swarming decks answered never a word; but one old tar on the *Hartford,* standing with lanyard in hand beside a great pivot-gun, so plain to view that you could see him smile, silently patted its big black breech and blandly grinned."

Before this array of might, the civil authorities surrendered the city with surly reluctance. Part of the fleet then ran up the river and compelled the capitulation of equally defenseless Baton Rouge and Natchez. For an exuberant moment it seemed that the navy alone could seize every Confederate point on the lower river. But when Farragut probed at fortified Vicksburg, he encountered an implacable resolve to fight. Federal operations on the river temporarily came to a halt. The Confederates, warned of coming events, hastened to strengthen their works at Vicksburg and Port Hudson.

Still, in the campaign just closed the Federals had achieved a lustrous success. They had closed off the mouth of the river to Confederate commerce and grasped the South's largest city, an important banking and industrial center. And holding New Orleans and south Louisiana, they had a base for possible future operations in the West.

Even in a top hat, Senator James H. Lane, who led the "Kansas Brigade" in the West, was barely taller than his rifle. Called a political "chameleon," Lane was a Democrat-turned-Republican who first was equivocal about slavery but later became an ardent "crusader for freedom." Characteristically, as a general he pillaged Union and Confederate property alike.

Sprawling, violent conflict at sea

T HE Confederacy," one analyst has written, "was not shot to death. It was strangled to death." The executioner was the United States Navy, which clamped an increasingly effective blockade on the long Southern coastline. Desperately needed supplies could not reach the South; cash crops could not get out. That was not the only blow the North's seamen struck. They landed armies on Virginia and Carolina beaches; they deprived the South of the Mississippi's mouth by their conquest of New Orleans and they helped take the rest of the river with a spectacular operation at Vicksburg.

The outnumbered Confederates fought back courageously. Daring blockade-runners slipped through the Union net. Southern warships, wooden and iron-clad alike, gave battle to the Union navy—at Hampton Roads, New Orleans, Mobile Bay. Rebel raiders traveled halfway around the world in search of Northern merchantmen. The best of these raiders was the *Alabama*, whose dashing captain *(below)* presided over the destruction of 58 Union vessels. But the *Alabama* met her match in the chain-armored *Kearsarge;* in a furious one-hour battle off the French coast *(right)* she was battered into the sea.

VICTORIOUS CAPTAIN of the *Alabama*, Raphael Semmes leans jauntily on a gun. Buoyed by repeated triumphs, he declared just before meeting the *Kearsarge:* "Defeat is impossible."

VANQUISHED RAIDER, the *Alabama (opposite, right)* exchanges fire with her foe shortly before sinking. The impressionist Edouard Manet, a spectator, painted this scene of the battle.

Baptism in battle for seagoing monsters of metal

WOODEN VICTIM of an ironclad, U.S.S. *Cumberland (left)* is sunk by the *Merrimack*. The victor was a former Union ship, renamed *Virginia* by the South but remembered by her original name.

THOUGH the French had launched the first ironclad warship in 1859 and the Union navy ultimately had scores of them, it was the South that put seagoing armor to the first test. At the start of the war the Confederates armored a floating battery at Fort Sumter and later fitted out a ship with an ironclad spear, called a ram, that pierced the U.S.S. *Richmond* on the Mississippi.

Then, on March 8, 1862, the Rebels sent into action the historic *Merrimack*—first ironclad to do battle. Day and night, 1,500 workers had labored to armor the massive, wheezing monster with flattened railroad tracks. In her first spectacular day of action she put three U.S. ships out of action in Hampton Roads.

But her triumph was short-lived. The very next day she met the Union's first ironclad, the tiny *Monitor*, and was held to a standstill. The *Monitor* introduced the revolving gun turret, though designer John Ericsson claimed no originality. "I believe it was known among the Greeks," he said. Though indecisive, the *Merrimack-Monitor* fight tolled the death knell of wooden warships.

A CLASH OF IRONCLADS results in a standoff as the *Monitor* (*foreground*) engages the *Merrimack* at close range. The Rebel vessel, unable to bring all its guns to bear, finally withdrew.

TWIN TURRETS of the *Onondaga* (*below*) exemplify the refinements of the Union monitors constructed after the success of the original *Monitor*. This late-comer saw action in mid-1864.

Porter's fleet sails past Vicksburg to join Grant, losing but one ship, the "Henry Clay" (left). The admiral risked the nocturnal passage as

HELPED BY HIGH WATER, three Union gunboats shell Fort Henry on the Tennessee River. Heavy rains flooded the fort but they also hampered Grant's army, which became mired.

Union teamwork on the rivers of the South

T HE river warfare conducted by the North offered, at its best, an unparalleled example of interservice cooperation. One of its chief beneficiaries was General U. S. Grant. Federal gunboats under him captured Fort Henry on the Tennessee River early in 1862; 18 months later, naval support enabled him to seize the war's greatest single prize: control of the Mississippi.

The key to the Mississippi was the city of Vicksburg. Grant's army moved south of the city and across from it. Now he required naval transport across the river—but Admiral David Porter's ships were above the city. Porter snaked his fleet down the river through a gantlet of Confederate fire, ferried Grant across, and then turned his guns on Rebel fortifications. Vicksburg fell on July 4. But some months later, when Porter tried to combine forces with the ineffectual politician-general Nathaniel Banks on the Red River, near disaster resulted.

Vicksburg citizens were attending a ball, but Confederate gunners detected the fleet and set buildings afire to illuminate their targets.

HINDERED BY LOW WATER, Porter's fleet, exposed by the defeat of General Banks, makes good its retreat, gingerly passing over the rapids near Alexandria, Louisiana. First tempted to scuttle his two-million-dollar fleet, Porter embraced a daring plan by an engineer officer who put thousands of men to work felling trees and in 10 days built a dam that raised the waters.

A RAM, the Rebel *Palmetto State (left)* destroys a Northern blockader by burying its prow in the foe's hull and firing its forward gun. Frank Vizetelly, noted artist of the Rebellion, drew this scene.

A SUBMARINE, the South's *Hunley*, only 35 feet in length and 5½ feet tall, awaits action in Charleston *(right)*. Eight men operating hand cranks propelled the clumsy vessel at four miles an hour.

Southerners at sea: valiant feats of the Rebel navy

NOT all the naval successes were scored by the North. Southern sailors displayed ingenuity and courage throughout the war, particularly in contending with the blockade. One of the most successful blockade-runners was Captain Robert B. Pegram, who slipped his *Nashville* through Federal traps time after time. Northerners cried for the dismissal of Navy Secretary Gideon Welles after the *Nashville*, having carried tons of munitions from England to Beaufort, North Carolina, deftly made her way back to sea despite Union efforts to bottle her up. The South also broke the blockade by brute force: on January 31, 1863, the Rebel navy sent two ironclads smashing through the Union line at Charleston.

One of the most spectacular Rebel exploits occurred when a Southern crew scored history's first submarine triumph. Horace L. Hunley, the sub's designer, earlier had perished during trial runs; so had several crews. Nevertheless brave crewmen took her into Charleston Harbor, poked her "torpedo" (a mine attached to the end of a spar) against the sloop *Housatonic*—and then went down with their victim in the explosion that followed.

A SIDE-WHEELER, the Confederate *Nashville* (*left*) sets the Union's *Harvey Birch* afire in the English Channel. The victor later freed the *Birch's* 32 crewmen in England.

"Damn the torpedoes!" at Mobile Bay

In the final summer of the war, Admiral David G. Farragut led a powerful fleet against the South's last major Gulf port, Mobile, a great center of blockade-running activity. Although 180 mines—called torpedoes—had been sown in the bay, Farragut refused to be intimidated. "Damn the torpedoes!" he cried, and sailed his wooden flagship, the *Hartford*, safely through the mines. Climbing into the rigging, Farragut directed his fleet in the furious action that followed. At close range, the *Hartford* exchanged broadsides with the powerful Rebel ironclad *Tennessee*. The two ships actually brushed in passing, as shown here. But soon the *Tennessee* was the only Confederate ship still in action and at last, badly damaged and out of control, she gave up the unequal fight. Mobile Bay was now in Union hands, and the day of the blockade-runner was virtually past.

48

3. THE CRITICAL CAMPAIGNS

ALL through the winter months of 1861-1862, the area around Washington resounded to the tramp of marching men. The government had assembled an army of 150,000 troops, at the time the largest military force ever brought together on American soil. Everybody expected that this mighty host would soon capture Richmond. To command it, President Lincoln named a rising young officer considered by many to be the best general on either side: 35-year-old George B. McClellan, whom the press hailed as the "Young Napoleon."

The previous summer McClellan had made a name for himself in the Union-sympathizing mountain counties of western Virginia. A small army under his direction had entered the area from Ohio, defeated a Confederate defending force and prepared the way for an eventual larger occupation. By his successful drive McClellan had deprived the Confederates of a potential base for offensive operations against the Northwest, and by "liberating" the mountain people he had won a significant propaganda victory, both for the Union and for himself.

McClellan was to prove the most puzzling and controversial general of the war. In person and manner, he radiated martial greatness. He was of average height, but he was so stockily built that he appeared shorter than he was. He was so muscular that he could bend a quarter over the end of his thumb with the pressure of his first and second fingers or toss a 200-pound man over his head. Handsome and regular of feature, he seemed, especially when astride

HEROES OF THE CONFEDERACY, Generals Robert E. Lee (*left*) and Stonewall Jackson plan the battle of Chancellorsville, the brilliant victory that cost Jackson his life.

a horse, to be the very embodiment of the qualities that make a general great.

The brilliant promise of McClellan was never fulfilled. His one great merit was that he was a superb trainer of troops. The fine Federal army in the East, the Army of the Potomac, was his creation. But he almost broke up when he had to send into combat the men he had trained. For one thing, he loved them too much to risk them in battle. "Every poor fellow that is killed or wounded almost haunts me," he confided to his wife. His greatest victories, he later boasted, were Manassas and Yorktown, two places he occupied virtually without loss of life—because the Confederates had evacuated them. His worst failing was that he lived in a world of his own making, a world filled with enemies who were forever about to destroy him. Some of them were men in his own government, but the most dangerous was the Confederate army, which he always saw at least twice life-size. During the winter months when it lay at Manassas, for example, it actually had 50,000 men, but McClellan insisted it had 100,000.

T HIS inability to grasp reality marked his strategic planning for operations in the spring of 1862. He announced that he had a plan to end the war at one stroke. He would move his army by water to the mouth of the Rappahannock River and up that stream a short distance to Urbana. There, standing between Richmond and Joseph E. Johnston's army at Manassas, he could either destroy the Confederates as they shifted south or occupy their capital. The merits of moving on Richmond by water, as he explained them to Lincoln, were that he would have a shorter land route to traverse and a secure line of communications protected by the navy.

In theory, the plan was excellent, but it ignored all political realities. Lincoln, as the nation's leader, was properly sensitive about the safety of Washington; the proposed movement would uncover the capital to possible attack from the Confederates poised at Manassas. Besides, asked the President, why go down to the Rappahannock in search of a fight when the enemy army was only 30 miles distant? McClellan argued that his move would force Johnston to move to meet him and that victory by his plan was certain. Anyway, he added, he would leave enough men behind him to make Washington safe. He finally won the President's grudging assent. Then the Confederates rudely upset the whole arrangement. Johnston, anticipating some kind of advance by the Federals and deeming Manassas a faulty defensive base, pulled his army back to the Rappahannock. Now the Urbana plan was out.

McClellan always found it hard to give up a plan, even when the situation that called it into being changed before his eyes. Instead of abandoning the plan he altered it: If he could not use the Rappahannock, he would resort to another route. He proposed that his army should be moved by ship to Fort Monroe on the point between the York and James Rivers known as the Peninsula, about 75 miles from the rebel capital. From there he would move his columns toward Richmond. Lincoln agreed to the altered plan, but again with reluctance.

In March, McClellan and his army finally departed Washington. But he did not leave behind as many men to protect the city as he had promised; moreover, instead of explaining the situation to the President in person, he waited until he got on board ship and then sent a note. When the President learned that Washington was inadequately defended, he promptly ordered

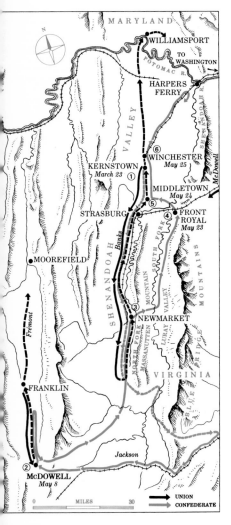

THE VALLEY CAMPAIGN:
FIRST PHASE

Stonewall Jackson's Shenandoah Valley Campaign of 1862 (above and on the opposite page) was one of the war's most dazzling exploits. Racing up and down the valley, he harassed a superior adversary and tied up thousands of Union troops needed elsewhere. After one of Banks's divisions gave him his only defeat, at Kernstown (1), the Rebel general headed south and overcame Frémont at McDowell (2). Then, unexpectedly, Jackson veered east at Newmarket (3), took a garrison at Front Royal (4), descended on Banks at Middletown (5) and crushed him at Winchester (6).

McDowell's corps of 30,000, about to embark, to remain south of Washington.

Still, McClellan began his operation with an army that numbered close to 100,000. It was a tremendous feat to move an army of that size the 200 miles to Fort Monroe. The 405 vessels of the Union fleet carried not only the troops but 14,000 horses and mules, over 4,000 wagons, 343 artillery pieces and some 600,000 rations; it was clear that the military services were converting rapidly to the requirements of large-scale war.

McClellan found only 11,000 Gray troops defending Yorktown. They held a strongly fortified line, however, and while McClellan paused before it, Johnston had time to reach the scene from the Rappahannock. Then McClellan decided to resort to the certain and comfortable method of siege to capture Yorktown. The Confederates held him off for a month, then retired up the line of the York.

Both President Davis and his military adviser, General Lee, expected that Johnston would contest closely the Federal advance. To their dismay Johnston announced that his strategy would be to continue to fall back. Then, near the gates of Richmond, when the Federals were far from their base, he would turn and destroy them. It was theoretically a feasible plan, but if it failed some vital territory would have been given up for no purpose.

Even against only token opposition, McClellan advanced with caution. Continually he begged Lincoln to order McDowell to join him. Although McDowell was only a two-day march away, McClellan characteristically insisted that he had to come by water, which would require more than a week. The President finally agreed to let McDowell join McClellan, but by land—thus keeping him in position to cover Washington.

The Confederate high command knew of McDowell's projected movement, and with anxious haste devised a plan to keep him near Washington. In the Shenandoah Valley, a convenient route to Washington, there was a small army under Stonewall Jackson, who was making such a reputation for mobility that his troops were becoming known as "Jackson's 'foot cavalry.'" Jackson received reinforcements that brought his strength to 17,000 men and was directed to give the impression that he meant to drive on Washington.

Jackson had his work cut out for him. Approaching the Valley from the west was a Federal column of perhaps 10,000, the vanguard of a larger force under Major General John C. Frémont. Near Winchester there was another army of 20,000 commanded by Major General Nathaniel P. Banks. Jackson performed brilliantly. He first attacked Frémont and pushed him back. Then he struck savagely at Banks and defeated him. Banks fled northward so precipitately that he had to leave behind large quantities of his supplies; hungry Confederates gratefully dubbed him "Commissary" Banks. Jackson followed him right to the Potomac crossings.

In official Washington, Jackson's approach excited some apprehension. Lincoln, however, saw in the situation an opportunity to trap the bold raider. He ordered Frémont to return to the Valley, Banks to move southward, and McDowell with his 30,000 men, just about to march to McClellan, to come in from the east. Jackson promptly pulled back. He just escaped the jaws of the trap as they were closing—and in parting paused to deliver sharp blows at the advance units of both Frémont and McDowell.

The Valley Campaign was a spectacular exploit. In two weeks Jackson had

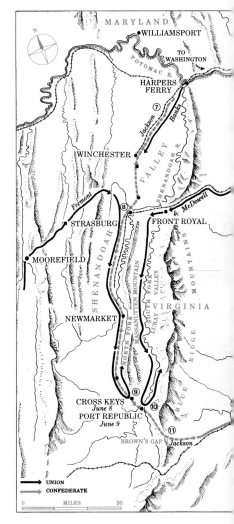

THE VALLEY CAMPAIGN:
SECOND PHASE

The bellicose Jackson, standing at the head of the Shenandoah Valley (7), threatened Washington, 50 miles away. Lincoln prepared a trap. He ordered Frémont to march east, McDowell to move west and Banks to drive Jackson south into the vise. But the wily Rebel outmaneuvered his foes. He slipped between Frémont and McDowell at Strasburg (8)—and then, when they gave chase, defeated Frémont at Cross Keys (9) and McDowell at Port Republic (10). Then he headed triumphantly for Brown's Gap (11) to entrain for the Peninsula and the Seven Days' battles.

marched 170 miles, routed two armies and held off 60,000 Federals. Outnumbered more than 3 to 1 in total forces, he had so arranged matters that he had fought on every occasion but one with the odds in his favor. Most important of all, he had altered the strategic picture before Richmond. McDowell's corps was so thoroughly exhausted by its hard march that it could not go to join McClellan. The "Young Napoleon" would have to do the job with the force he had.

At Richmond, Johnston finally delivered his heralded blow, striking McClellan's forces at Fair Oaks and Seven Pines. He accomplished nothing and in the fighting was so badly wounded that he had to give up the command. To succeed him Davis named Robert E. Lee. Few realized that the South's greatest soldier was about to make a sensational emergence.

Immediately Lee christened his forces the Army of Northern Virginia. The title was revealing. Lee meant to return the war to northern Virginia, to the frontier of the Confederacy. He was a natural field commander, courageous and combative. He now wished not merely to drive McClellan from before Richmond but to destroy him.

L EE thought he saw in the arrangement of the Federal army an opportunity to accomplish his purpose. Two thirds of McClellan's army lay south of the Chickahominy River, a stream which flowed in front of Richmond to the James, and one corps north of it. Lee learned of this from his dashing cavalry leader, "Jeb" Stuart, who rode completely around the Federal army to secure the information. Stuart also reported that the weak right wing was "in the air," that is, not anchored to any natural obstacle, and thus vulnerable. Now Lee matured his plan. He would swiftly and secretly bring Jackson from the Valley, raising his force to 85,000. He would mass the bulk of his troops, 56,000, opposite the Federal right and attack and chew it up. Then, he believed, the rest of the Blue army would attempt to retreat along the York River to its base, and he could follow and smash it. It was a brilliant plan and also a plan that contained serious dangers. He would have to leave only a small force confronting McClellan's main array south of the Chickahominy. McClellan might even slip past Lee and take Richmond. Lee reasoned that in the excitement McClellan would think only of his safety. The Confederate read his opponent's character perfectly. McClellan reported apprehensively to Washington that he was about to be attacked by an enemy numbering 200,000.

When Lee's plans were complete, he struck. But the battles of the Seven Days, fought between June 26 and July 2, did not go at all as Lee planned. He damaged the detached Federal right wing but could not destroy it. New to the ways of large command and lacking an adequate staff, Lee was unable to control his army. In the first onslaught he succeeded in putting only 14,000 of his 56,000 men into action. Nor did McClellan fall back along the York line. The Federal commander was badly shaken, but this time he reacted with desperate vigor. He pulled his army together and, abandoning his base on the York, retired south to the James, where the navy was to set up a new base for him. Lee followed and thrust savagely, again and again. Each attack failed—McClellan conducted his withdrawal with skill, and Lee still had trouble concentrating his troops. Both armies suffered severe casualties, but Lee's were heavier and more damaging. McClellan had lost 15,000 men; of these, 10,000 were prisoners and would eventually be exchanged. Lee's losses were

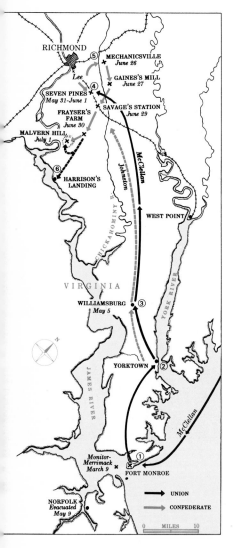

UNION FAILURE
ON THE PENINSULA

In March 1862, Federal forces under McClellan arrived by sea at Fort Monroe (1). After besieging Yorktown (2), McClellan followed the withdrawing Johnston toward Richmond; en route they fought inconclusively at Williamsburg (3). On May 31 the Rebels attacked unsuccessfully at Seven Pines (4). Then at Mechanicsville (5), Lee, replacing Johnston, launched the series of blows known as the Seven Days' battles. This effort to destroy McClellan did not succeed, but the Federals reeled back to Harrison's Landing (6), where they finally embarked for Washington, their campaign a failure.

20,000, but 11,000 of them would never return—they were killed or died of wounds.

At the end of the Seven Days, McClellan was at Harrison's Landing on the James and on a safe line of water communications. Even now he was only 25 miles from Richmond. But instead of resuming the drive on the Rebel capital, the Federal high command in Washington decided to evacuate the army by sea to northern Virginia and join it to a smaller force already there under Major General John Pope. The combined armies would then move under Mc-Clellan's command against Richmond on the overland route. As the Federals prepared to leave the Peninsula, they could not possibly dream that it would be two bloody years before they would again stand this close to Richmond.

The Southern commander watched the Union moves with fascination. He soon divined that the Federals were pulling back from Richmond. The division of the Federal forces offered him an opportunity too inviting to be ignored. Lee decided to race northward and smash Pope before he could be joined by McClellan. Lee's strategy was, as always, audacious; he left only a small force to watch the remaining Federals. If McClellan should decide to be bold and ignore orders, he could walk into Richmond. Lee trusted correctly that McClellan would not act.

The man who was really in a dangerous situation was John Pope. His army, created by combining the three separate units that had faced Jackson in the Valley, numbered about 45,000 men. They had little confidence in Pope, who had been brought in from the West. He was a man of striking appearance and he liked to fight. But he had McClellan's talent for unreality in reverse— where the Young Napoleon saw dangers that did not exist, Pope did not see those that did. He boasted too much of what he would do to the Confederates, and one of his effusions infuriated his men. He had come from the West, he said, and there he was accustomed to seeing the backs of the enemy. In the East he had heard too much talk about strategy and lines of retreat. "Let us study the probable lines of retreat for our opponents," he urged, "and leave our own to take care of themselves." He was also supposed to have said, although he denied it, that his headquarters would be in the saddle, which caused Confederate wags to quip that his headquarters were where his hindquarters ought to be.

N ow, maneuvering below the Rappahannock, Pope suddenly found himself facing stronger opposition. He retired north of the river. At the same time, the Federal high command sensed the danger and spurred McClellan to rush his arriving troops forward to Pope. McClellan complied, but neither he nor his corps generals showed any great sense of urgency about the crisis. There was much ill feeling between McClellan and Pope; some of McClellan's officers, indeed, seemed to consider Pope a far more dangerous enemy than Lee.

While the Federal armies were moving to an uneasy concentration, Lee crossed the Rappahannock to bring Pope to bay. The Confederate commander sent Jackson on a long, fast flanking march to the left that brought him to Pope's rear; Stonewall's soldiers fell with delight on a Union supply dump and enjoyed a day of looting that was talked about in the Army of Northern Virginia for the rest of the war. Lee followed with the rest of the army.

When Pope discovered there was an enemy force behind him, he swung

A pioneer "aircraft carrier" was the Union's "George Washington Parke Custis," which raised an observation balloon to search for Confederate vessels on the Potomac. The South also launched at least one balloon, which General James Longstreet called "a great patchwork ship of many and varied hues"—reputedly made out of the silk dresses of Confederate ladies.

back to find it. He came upon Jackson in the general area of Manassas. Although he knew that a single Gray corps would not be there unless it expected support, he convinced himself that he could destroy it before help arrived. He opened the battle of Second Bull Run, or Second Manassas, on August 29. He had about 80,000 men and a heavy numerical superiority. But while he was wasting his strength in piecemeal attacks, Lee linked up with Jackson, giving the Confederates a force of 55,000. On August 30 Pope continued his assaults. Suddenly Lee threw Longstreet's whole corps forward in a crushing counterattack that swept the Federals from the field. The stunned Blue army reeled back in a withdrawal that soon degenerated into a demoralized retreat. It was not just the Confederate blow that did it—the men had never believed that Pope was competent, and now they knew it and did not want to fight under him any longer.

Pope had to order his forces to retire to the Washington defenses. As the beaten troops stumbled to safety Pope came upon Brigadier General Samuel D. Sturgis, one of McClellan's commanders, still on the road with his troops. "Too late, Sammy, too late," Pope cried reproachfully. Sturgis snarled back: "I always told you that if they gave you rope enough you would hang yourself!" The McClellan clique had not consciously wanted Pope to fail, but it could not be said that they had shown any driving desire for his success. Such dark feuds would have ruined the best army in the world, and the force that finally reached the Washington fortifications was not at the moment an army. It was a shapeless mass of two armies, McClellan's and Pope's, and it needed a leader whom it could trust.

The condition of the army dictated Lincoln's choice. Pope was obviously out; he was relieved and sent west to a minor assignment. Lincoln had decided that McClellan was unfit for field command, and he was indignant at the Young Napoleon's treatment of Pope. But he knew that McClellan was the only man who could reorganize the troops. "If he can't fight himself," the President observed, "he excels in making others ready to fight." So Lincoln named him commander of all the forces in the Washington defenses—but before operations were resumed Lincoln meant to find another general.

Abruptly Lee upset Lincoln's plans. In early September the Confederate army crossed the Potomac and invaded Maryland. Lee wanted to get the war out of Virginia during the harvest season to insure the gathering of vitally needed crops, and he thought that the presence of his army might be the impelling cause that would bring Maryland to secede. He hoped too for a victory that might be followed by an advance into Pennsylvania. Lincoln could not switch commanders at this juncture, and so, with misgivings, he directed McClellan to meet the threat posed by Lee.

As the young general moved across Maryland, he had a rare stroke of luck. A Confederate order found in a field revealed that the Gray army was divided. One part of it under Jackson had gone to gobble up a Federal garrison at Harpers Ferry. McClellan was exultant. He exclaimed: "Here is a paper with which if I cannot whip Bobbie Lee, I will be willing to go home." McClellan pushed forward with what for him was headlong celerity. But his notions of mobility were peculiarly his own. Actually, his advance was fairly deliberate, and when he finally came up with Lee he wasted a whole day in surveying the Confederate line of defense.

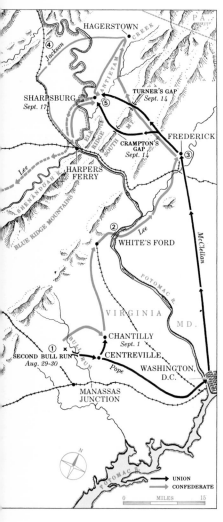

A REBEL INVASION
BLOCKED AT ANTIETAM

After Second Bull Run (1) and a skirmish at Chantilly, Lee boldly invaded Maryland, crossing the Potomac at White's Ford (2); the Federals under McClellan followed cautiously. At Frederick (3), McClellan learned Lee had sent Jackson (4) to Harpers Ferry, and he hurried to attack Lee's reduced army. After sharp fighting at Crampton's and Turner's Gaps, the armies met near Sharpsburg (5) in the savage battle of Antietam. A Southern disaster was prevented by the arrival of the forces from Harpers Ferry—but the invasion had failed, and Lee retreated.

Lee took up a position behind Antietam Creek near the town of Sharpsburg. He had come into Maryland with perhaps 50,000 troops—many Confederates simply refused to fight in the North and dropped off to return later—but some of his units were still hurrying from Harpers Ferry to rejoin him. With this thin array Lee had to hold off 87,000 Federals.

On September 17 McClellan attacked. He threw three consecutive heavy blows at the Confederate line, hitting first the left, then the center and finally the right. The fighting was murderous and the Confederate ranks sagged before each onslaught. Each time they almost broke; each time they miraculously held. Then, late in the afternoon, the last assault on the right seemed on the point of crashing through. Lee was desperate. He looked anxiously down the road that led to Harpers Ferry. Suddenly he saw A. P. Hill's division toiling forward. Hill, clad in his customary red battle shirt, rode up and down the line, whipping laggards onward with his sword. Before the war he and McClellan had been rivals for the same girl. McClellan had won her, and it was said that because of this Hill fought against McClellan with a special ferocity. Something drove him on to a special effort on this day. His men rushed into the faltering line—and in furious fighting repelled the attack.

Probably McClellan could still have had the victory if he had put in his reserve. But he could not bring himself to take the decisive risk. He halted the battle. The next day the two armies watched each other in sullen expectancy. When McClellan made no further move, Lee retired to Virginia. Ten thousand Confederates had been killed and wounded in the fighting, and 12,000 Federals. Men would remember Antietam as the bloodiest single day of the war.

As Lee withdrew to Virginia, McClellan attempted no pursuit; he said that he could not advance until he had more men, more supplies, more of everything. Lincoln made a visit to McClellan's camp to determine the general's purposes. One night Lincoln stood with a friend looking over the vast expanse of tents. Suddenly the President asked his companion what they were viewing. Surprised, the man said he supposed it was the Army of the Potomac. "So it is called," Lincoln replied bitterly, "but that is a mistake; it is only McClellan's bodyguard."

Not until the end of October did McClellan stir; by then Lincoln had had more than enough. He relieved McClellan from command, this time for good. To old Frank Blair, the father of Postmaster General Montgomery Blair, who came to plead for McClellan's retention, Lincoln said with finality: "He has got the 'slows,' Mr. Blair."

To succeed McClellan, Lincoln named one of his corps commanders, Ambrose E. Burnside. Twice before, Lincoln had offered Burnside the command—in the summer and just before Antietam. Each time Burnside had refused on the ground he lacked competence. Now it was practically thrust upon him, and he had to accept.

The commander was a large man, with bushy and distinctive facial adornments; he would add his name to the language as "burnsides" or "sideburns." He had been a good subordinate officer. But, as he himself was so pathetically aware, he did not have the ability to direct a large army. The campaign he would immediately inaugurate cruelly revealed his deficiencies.

When Burnside took command, the army was in northwestern Virginia. He

Union General Ambrose Burnside served after the war as a senator from Rhode Island. He was not noted for his intellect, but his impressive bearing pleased the voters. "I know there is nothing weighty behind that grand manner," admitted one Providence lady, "but what a treasure he is, after all."

The bombastic General John Pope, defeated at Second Bull Run, was hampered both by his high opinion of himself and by the low opinion in which others held him. General McClellan's wife called him "that puppy," and General Samuel Sturgis said acidly: "I don't care for John Pope a pinch of owl dung."

decided to move it eastward and cross the Rappahannock River at Fredericksburg. From here he would drive straight south at Richmond. The plan might conceivably have worked if Burnside had got to Fredericksburg before Lee could shift to meet him. The Federal advance reached the crossing first, but pontoon bridges ordered by Burnside had not arrived. Instead of throwing a force over to seize Fredericksburg as a bridgehead, Burnside waited for the pontoons. By the time he received them Lee's whole army stood waiting on the other side.

Having lost the element of surprise, Burnside might well have called off his offensive. He had 120,000 men to Lee's 80,000, but the terrain in and around Fredericksburg, crowned by hills, constituted a natural fortification. Besides, it was mid-December, and even if Burnside broke Lee's lines he would not have much time left for active campaigning. But he thought that he had been put in to fight, and fight he would. On the 13th he crossed the river; Lee waited to receive the attack. The Confederate front ran for seven miles, and it was least formidable below Fredericksburg. But Burnside chose to deliver his main assault on the town. Here he had to fight through a narrow, cramped area before he could even approach the key Confederate position, a stone wall at the base of a hill. Again and again his men flung themselves forward in bloody and hopeless charges. As fast as one brigade was cut down, a Federal general reported, "the next brigade coming up in succession would do its duty and melt like snow coming down on warm ground."

Burnside was desperate as he witnessed the slaughter of his troops. He talked wildly about leading a last charge of his old corps, but his officers restrained him. He wept when he gave the order to withdraw over the river. He left on the field 12,000 dead and wounded. After the battle an officer found him pacing his tent in agony. "Those men over there!" he cried. "I am thinking of them all the time!"

In January 1863, tormented beyond endurance by his failure at Fredericksburg and the cruel criticisms of his subordinates, Burnside asked to be relieved. To succeed him Lincoln named "Fighting Joe" Hooker. Working his way up from brigade to corps command in the Eastern army, the tall, florid-faced Hooker had made a reputation for hard fighting and also for loud boasting and ambitious intriguing. Among other things, he had played a part in undermining his predecessor. Hooker had important political support in some Republican circles and he was considered to be one of the best of the corps commanders. Lincoln was aware of Hooker's personal faults and he knew about the general's loud talk, including a much-quoted statement that the country needed a dictator. In naming Hooker to the post, Lincoln wrote him an eloquent and moving letter of advice. He had heard about the dictator threat, he said, but was not angered by it. "Only those generals who gain successes can set up dictators," the President pointed out. "What I now ask of you is military success, and I will risk the dictatorship." Hooker read the document to a friend and burst out emotionally that it was the kind of letter a father would write to a son.

This quality of emotional extravagance was the key to Hooker's character. It invested him with a kind of juvenile charm, but it constituted his greatest weakness as a general. He lacked the power to dominate a situation. After he took over from Burnside, he brought the army, whose number had been de-

A Union telegrapher sends a message on a machine used by operators who did not know code. When they dialed a letter, a machine at the other end registered the same selection. A rising businessman named Andrew Carnegie helped organize the army telegraphers. Some 40 years later, millionaire Carnegie pensioned more than 100 Civil War telegraphers or their widows.

pleted by desertions after Fredericksburg, back to a size of 120,000 and up to a new peak of competence and morale. It was the finest army on the planet, he exclaimed, and it ought to be able to go to Richmond on its belly. "My plans are perfect," he announced to a gathering of his officers, "and when I start to carry them out, may God have mercy on General Lee, for I will have none."

This constant bragging revealed a gnawing inner uncertainty. Known as a heavy drinker, he abruptly stopped the habit upon assuming command. He drank to buttress his courage, and the sudden deprivation probably was not good for him.

With all his shortcomings, Hooker had one of the best strategic mentalities of the war. He brought this skill into play when he surveyed the situation around Fredericksburg. His army lay on the north side of the Rappahannock, and his problem was to get it across the river and at Lee without being led into the slaughter pen that had been Burnside's tragedy. He devised a brilliant operation. Leaving part of his force opposite Fredericksburg to hold Lee's attention, he moved a column 30 miles up the river, crossed, and brought it down on Lee's left. Not until the Federals were approaching the Confederate flank was Lee aware of the danger. Hooker had advanced through the desolate Virginia area of underbrush and scrub trees known as the Wilderness. Now all he had to do was to break out into the open country around Fredericksburg where he could maneuver. Then, teaming up with his second force opposite Fredericksburg, he could hold Lee in a crushing vise.

Hooker at his headquarters talked loudly about his achievement. But his boasting had a queer ring. "The rebel army is now the legitimate property of the Army of the Potomac," he cried. "They may as well pack up their haversacks and make for Richmond." It was as though he wanted the enemy to retreat without fighting. On May 1 he moved toward Fredericksburg. He seemed listless and detached from his own operation. He asked a staff officer to post the troops, saying: "My God, Warren, I know nothing of this ground." Suddenly in the darkly menacing woods he encountered Confederate troops.

When Lee awoke to the nature of the Federal movement, he acted with audacious vigor. Some of his men were on duty elsewhere; to deal with Hooker he could bring to bear only 42,000 troops. But he advanced boldly and struck the Federal van hard. This first touch of opposition seemed to collapse Hooker. He retired to the little village of Chancellorsville and announced to his generals that he had chosen to let the Confederates attack him. He had lost his nerve—and the initiative.

IT was clear to Lee that Hooker was an enemy with whom great risks could be taken. The Confederate commander resolved on a great risk to win a great objective—the destruction of the Federal army. He and Jackson evolved a plan. Jackson would make a wide march to the west and come in with a surprise attack on Hooker's right while Lee engaged Fighting Joe's attention on his front. Jackson proposed that his corps be strengthened to 28,000 for a killing blow. It was a breath-taking idea, for it would leave Lee with only 14,000 to confront 70,000 Federals. Lee thought a moment. "Well, go on," he said. "Old Jack" set out on his march.

Jackson's sweeping movement took most of the day and was visible to the Federals. The information that he was on the move was passed along, but it made no impression on the command generals on the right or on Hooker. Near

At the war's start, Rebel cavalrymen like this dashing fellow rode their own blooded mounts and far outclassed Union horsemen. But as time passed, Northern horsemanship improved while Southern troops and horses alike grew exhausted. Yankee cavalry also benefited from a horseshoe machine, much coveted by Rebel spies, which turned out 60 horseshoes a minute.

dusk the soldiers noted that many deer were running through the woods. Then a blast of rifle fire cut through the trees—and suddenly Jackson's ragged men hurtled forward in a screaming charge.

The attack rolled up the Federal right. But gradually the Bluecoats rallied and set up a defense line. With darkness falling, Jackson raged forward. Crashing through the woods near the fighting front he was mistakenly shot by his own men. His wounds were so serious that he had to be carried to the rear.

The next day Hooker shortened his lines, which enabled the Confederate wings to draw together. His troops, in a constricted position, took a severe pounding, especially from Confederate artillery fire, but they held their line. By shifting units from Fredericksburg, Hooker increased his strength up to over 80,000. He might well have gone over to the offensive, broken out, and defeated Lee. His corps commanders joined in urging him to attack. But the fight had gone out of him. He had, moreover, suffered an accident—on the 3rd, a Confederate solid shot had thrown the pillar of a house against him and knocked him senseless. Although he revived, he seemed dazed. On May 5 he ordered a return to the north side of the river.

Lee had marked up another dazzling success. But he had failed again to destroy the Federal army. His cost in casualties was heavy, over 10,000 men. Most serious of all, he had lost his ablest lieutenant. Jackson's wounded arm had to be amputated. On May 10 he died from the effects of complicating pneumonia. "Stonewall" became a myth in the Army of Northern Virginia. The soldiers loved to tell of the angel who was sent down to bear Jackson's soul to heaven. The angel searched everywhere for the body but could not find it and came back to report that he had failed. On reaching heaven he found the object of his hunt already there. Jackson had outflanked the angel.

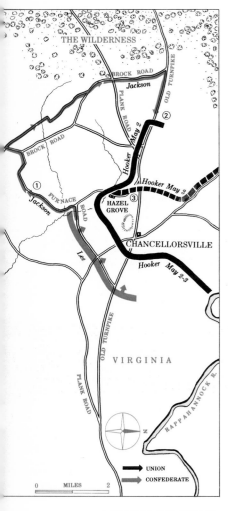

A BOLD FLANK ATTACK
AT CHANCELLORSVILLE

Facing a superior Northern force under Hooker at Chancellorsville, Lee made one of the most daring moves of the war. He sent Jackson and 28,000 men on a long flanking march (1) around Hooker's right while for hours he boldly confronted the 70,000 Federals with only 14,000 men. Late that day Jackson fell on the Union flank (2). Hooker's men were routed, but Jackson was fatally injured. As darkness fell the Union forces rallied at Hazel Grove (3) and held (broken line). The next day Hooker—though facing a divided, inferior enemy—began to withdraw.

W HILE Federal efforts in the East were encountering frustrating failures, the Northern armies in the West continued to mark up successes. After the fall of Corinth, Halleck was called to Washington to become general in chief. Before he left, he wrote a directive that revealed the traditional cast of Northern military thinking. Grant, the hardest-fighting Northern general yet to appear, but careless in manner and dress, was given the relatively unimportant work of guarding railroad communications in western Tennessee and northern Mississippi. Buell, who had no experience in commanding in combat but was all spit and polish, was awarded a vital combat objective, to capture Chattanooga on the Tennessee River line. He set up a base at Nashville and prepared his offensive. Like McClellan, he did everything slowly. Before he could advance, his opponent, Braxton Bragg, seized the initiative from him.

When Bragg had succeeded Beauregard as commander in the West, his army had been at Tupelo in northern Mississippi. He had brought it the 776 miles to Chattanooga in a vast rail movement that had required most of two months and the services of six lines. The beetle-browed, sour-mannered Bragg was determined to return the war to Kentucky and perhaps to invade the Northwest. He possessed some of the qualities of a great strategist. He decided to strike suddenly northward into Kentucky while a smaller Confederate army under Edmund Kirby Smith at Cumberland Gap marched to join him. The Confederate move would force Buell to follow, thus breaking his grip on Tennessee. Moreover, the Confederates would stand between Buell and his base at Louisville. They could force him to fight on ground of their choosing. If they smashed Buell, the entire frontier of the Ohio River would lie open before them.

It was a brilliant scheme, and at first it seemed to be working. Bragg got his movement off on time—it coincided with Lee's invasion of Maryland—and he beat Buell to Kentucky, where Kirby Smith joined him. But as Buell approached, Bragg made no effort to prevent him from entering Louisville. At the critical moment Bragg had grown cautious.

Buell reorganized his army in Louisville and then came out looking for Bragg. The two armies met at the battle of Perryville on October 8. It was an indecisive engagement, a kind of shoving match, but at the end it was Bragg who yielded the field. He retired to Tennessee, and Buell returned slowly to Nashville. Buell's lethargic pursuit was too much for Lincoln. He removed Buell at about the same time he got rid of McClellan. Another general with the "slows" had been eliminated.

To replace Buell, Lincoln named William S. Rosecrans, who had made a good reputation as a fighter under McClellan and Grant. "Old Rosy" was a volatile and colorful man, who would pass in an instant from anger to affection and from optimism to pessimism. He had shown that he was an aggressive soldier and a good strategist. What he had not yet revealed was an almost total lack of balance and poise.

At first Rosecrans seemed to be another Buell. At Nashville he organized his forces and called constantly and stridently for more men and more supplies. Not until near the end of the year did Rosecrans and Bragg, both urged on by their governments, advance to seek battle. The two armies met on December 31 at the battle of Murfreesboro, or Stones River, Tennessee. It was Bragg who attacked, although the Federals had a slight numerical advantage, probably 45,000 to 37,000. The Confederate assault bent back the Union right but could not turn it. Bragg waited a day, then he hit the Federal left and failed again. His losses had been heavy, and at last he pulled back. Rosecrans held his line and the territory his advance had occupied. The Federals still had a long road ahead to Chattanooga, but at last they were moving.

Meanwhile the leader of the other Western army, U. S. Grant, who had been held inactive since Shiloh, secured permission from Washington to mount an offensive against Vicksburg, the key to the remaining Confederate defenses on the Mississippi.

He tried first to approach the city by land, moving south from Memphis. But the Confederates ripped at Grant's supply line so savagely that he had to abandon his advance. He adopted a new plan. He returned to Memphis and brought his whole army, supported by a strong naval force, down the river to a point above Vicksburg on the Louisiana side. From there he attempted to cross to the east side and strike at the city from the north.

Now began the first of a series of frustrating failures. The terrain above Vicksburg was low and marshy and crisscrossed by rivers and bayous. The army could not move in it, and even the navy could make little headway. The Confederates, under John C. Pemberton, a Pennsylvanian who had thrown in his lot with the South, repelled every thrust. At Grant's headquarters plans were discussed to cross below the city. It was thought that naval transports could not make the passage in front of the Rebel river batteries without destruction, and without the ships the army could not reach the east side. So

Union soldiers laboriously dug this canal across the river loop at Vicksburg in an effort to enable gunboats to get past the city without coming under fire from its cannon. The attempt was costly—and, as General Grant had anticipated, fruitless. Ironically, some years later the Mississippi, shifting course, bypassed Vicksburg by almost the same route.

thousands of men were set to work digging a canal where the river made a great bend at Vicksburg. When it was completed, it was found that not enough water flowed into it to float the fleet. Grant had little confidence that any of his moves would work. He had decided on another plan and was waiting for the right time to try it.

With the coming of spring Grant put his plan into execution. Acting Rear Admiral David D. Porter had agreed to try to run transports past Vicksburg, meet the army on the west bank below the city, and ferry it across to the east side. To distract Pemberton while this was happening, Grant sent a cavalry force under Colonel Benjamin Grierson plunging through Mississippi. Grierson slashed south, ripping up railroads and making himself as conspicuous as possible. He was supposed to meet Grant below Vicksburg, but he arrived before the army had crossed. With Gray pursuers hot on his heels, his one chance was to dash for the Union lines at Baton Rouge. He just made it to safety. His men had ridden 600 miles in 16 days and had thoroughly distracted Pemberton. It was one of the most successful cavalry raids of the war.

Meanwhile Porter had run his transports past the blazing river batteries. He met the army below the city and carried it across to the east side. At last Grant was on dry ground where he could move. And he moved with dazzling rapidity, completely confusing Pemberton. He first drove eastward, where a Rebel force menaced his rear, and defeated it at Raymond and Jackson. Next he swung back toward Vicksburg, smashing Pemberton at Champion's Hill and the Big Black River. Then he closed in on Vicksburg itself. He tried at first to storm the strong works, failed, and settled down to a siege.

It had been one of the most audacious campaigns of the war. Outnumbered, in 18 days Grant had marched 200 miles, won five battles, inflicted losses of nearly 12,000 men and 100 guns on the foe, and shut that foe up in his fortress. Now he had Vicksburg in an iron grip that only a miracle would loosen.

Pemberton held out for almost seven weeks. His soldiers and the people of the city, subjected to frequent attacks and constant shelling, endured the siege with desperate courage. Civilians took cover in hillside caves; as many as 25 people would crowd into one of the small shelters. "We are utterly cut off from the world, surrounded by a circle of fire," wrote one girl in her diary. Eventually food supplies ran short, and near-starvation conditions prevailed. Both soldiers and civilians were reduced to eating mule and horse meat.

The surrender came on July 4. Pemberton thought that if Grant could occupy the city on the national holiday, he would agree to parole the garrison of 30,000 men instead of sending them to Northern prisons. Grant paroled the men, but outraged Southerners charged that Yankee Pemberton had yielded on the 4th to give his Northern compatriots something to cheer about. Confederate troops would never again serve under him.

With the fall of Vicksburg, Port Hudson in Louisiana, the other remaining Confederate stronghold on the river, surrendered to a besieging force under General N. P. Banks. At last the Federals had control of the Mississippi. The Confederacy was now split into two parts and the Confederate states west of the river were isolated from the main war. "The Father of Waters again goes unvexed to the sea," said Lincoln in one of his memorable sentences.

It was one of the great turning points of the war. And on the other vital line in the West, the conflict was turning against the Confederacy. In that same

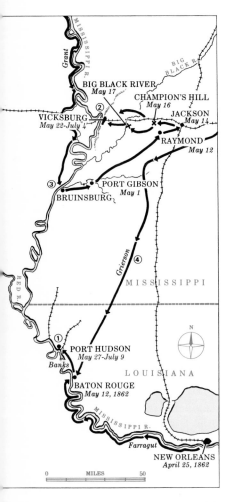

THE FALL OF VICKSBURG:
THE CONFEDERACY SPLIT

The capture of New Orleans and Baton Rouge left Port Hudson (1) and Vicksburg (2) the only Rebel strongholds on the Mississippi. Grant's all-out drive on Vicksburg began early in 1863. Gunboats ferried the Union troops to Bruinsburg (3) as Colonel Benjamin Grierson distracted the Rebels with a slashing raid on their rear (4). Grant, in a series of sharp engagements at Raymond, Jackson, Champion's Hill and Big Black River, drove the Confederates into Vicksburg, which he then besieged. The city fell on July 4. Port Hudson surrendered a few days later.

summer of 1863 Rosecrans resumed his advance toward Chattanooga and by skilled maneuvering forced Bragg farther back into east Tennessee. He completed the first phase of his movement by July 3 and then paused at Tullahoma to regroup. The Federals had the Mississippi line and now they were in position to drive at their next objective in the West, the Tennessee River line.

W HILE U. S. Grant was closing his ring around Vicksburg, the Confederate high command with desperate urgency was seeking ways to save the vital Mississippi fortress. The proposal most strongly advanced was to hold defensively in Virginia and send a part of Lee's army, preferably under Lee's command, to join Bragg in Tennessee and thus relieve pressure on Vicksburg. But Lee demurred. He did not know the ground in the West. He did not want to leave Virginia, which to him was the true seat of the war. He advanced a plan of his own: He would invade Pennsylvania. A successful offensive on Northern soil would do more than relieve Vicksburg, he argued. It would depress enemy morale, induce foreign intervention and perhaps even bring the war to a victorious conclusion.

Davis supported the proposal, and in June 75,000 Confederates left Fredericksburg, marched through the Valley and then headed north across the Potomac, into Maryland and Pennsylvania. Hooker, on the north side of the Rappahannock, studied the movement and made a strange proposal to Lincoln. With the Rebel army strung out as it was, he asked, could he not attack its rear at Fredericksburg? Back came a homely but vivid reply. Watch Lee's army, Lincoln advised, and forget about Fredericksburg: "I would not take any risk of being entangled upon the river, like an ox jumped half over a fence, and liable to be torn by dogs, front and rear, without a fair chance to gore one way or kick the other."

The Gray tide continued to flow northward, and five days later another dispatch from Hooker came to Lincoln. This one was fantastic. Now Fighting Joe wanted to ignore Lee and march on Richmond. Patiently the President delivered another lecture on military science. Lee's army and not Richmond was the real objective, he emphasized. Hooker should follow Lee's march on the "inside track" and fight him if the opportunity offered. "If he stays where he is," Lincoln added, "fret him and fret him."

Hooker was fretting himself more than his opponent. He did not want to meet again the man who had defeated him at Chancellorsville. Constantly he leveled complaints at Washington, and finally, when some troops he had requested were refused, he asked to be relieved. Lincoln appointed in his place George G. Meade, one of the corps commanders, solid and competent, better than McClellan but cast in the same traditional mold.

Meade took over, on June 28, at a critical moment—really, although he did not know it, on the eve of battle. The Confederate army was ahead of him, spread out in three columns. The Federal army of 90,000, moving on Lincoln's "inside track," was approaching the Rebels from the rear. Lee was unaware of this. When he started north, he had directed his cavalry leader, Jeb Stuart, to cover the army's right flank. But he had given Stuart discretion as to routes he could follow. Stuart, beplumed and gay, was a fine horseman. He was also somewhat juvenile, and he delighted in spectacular exploits, such as riding around Federal armies. He exercised his discretion so liberally that

Benjamin Grierson seemed an improbable candidate for heroism on horseback. A music teacher from Illinois who had written campaign songs for Lincoln, Grierson was afraid of horses. Assigned a cavalry command, he led a sensational raid behind Rebel lines and wrote his wife in astonishment: "I like Byron have had to wake up in the morning and find myself famous."

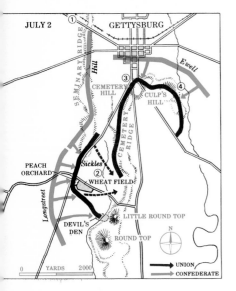

THE TURNING POINT
AT GETTYSBURG

On July 1 Meade's Union cavalry encountered one of Lee's divisions northwest of Gettysburg (1); in the resultant fighting the Federals drew back to the hills south of town. Next day Lee launched a series of attacks. Sickles' exposed Union corps (2) was forced back to Cemetery Ridge, where it held; Ewell struck the Union right at Cemetery (3) and Culp's (4) Hills without success. On July 3 (lower map), after another vain assault on Culp's Hill (5), Lee struck his final blow: Pickett's famous charge (6). When it failed, the battle was over; after a day Lee retreated.

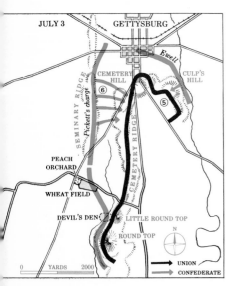

he put Hooker's army between him and his own and could not get back until July 2. Lee was without his "eyes."

When Lee at last discovered that the Federal army was coming up, he hastily issued orders to pull his scattered columns together. At the same time, Meade was uniting his marching corps, aware that Lee would attack if he could. Seeking the best position to receive the blow, Meade shifted toward the little road hub of Gettysburg. Lee, too, moved along the network of roads to Gettysburg. The two armies, much like blind wrestlers, were converging for the greatest battle ever fought on the North American continent.

THEY made contact on July 1. On that day the armies sparred for position. At the end the Confederates had pushed the Federals out of Gettysburg and onto a series of heights below the town. The Federal line was strong and in contour resembled an inverted fishhook. The right rested on Culp's Hill and Cemetery Hill, and the front stretched for three miles along Cemetery Ridge. At the other end of the ridge was an eminence, Little Round Top, a possible key to the Federal left and center. The Rebels lay in the town and opposite the Federal front on Seminary Ridge.

Units of both sides continued to stream in after darkness. In the Confederate camp Lee discussed plans with his corps commanders. The ablest of them, James Longstreet, argued that the Federal position was too strong to attack. Maneuver the Bluecoats out of it, he advised, and fight the battle elsewhere. Calmly Lee replied that he would attack. He was too committed to disengage, he said, and anyway he was confident of success. He would attack the Federal left with Longstreet's corps, while Richard S. Ewell's corps made a diversion on the right, at Culp's Hill. If the main assault succeeded, the third corps under A. P. Hill would come in to clinch the victory.

On July 2 Longstreet did not get his men into position to advance until the afternoon. He did not like this attack; after the war it would be charged that he had deliberately dragged his feet and so lost the battle. The truth was that he deployed his corps as quickly as possible. And even if he had delivered his onslaught in the morning, it would have met the same Federal strength as in the afternoon.

When the attack finally jumped off, it smashed into immediate opposition. The Federal corps commander on the left, Daniel Sickles, seeking higher ground, had rolled his corps forward. His position was thus stronger, but he had left a gap between him and the troops on his right. The Confederates punched through Sickles in hard fighting, and some of them veered toward Little Round Top. Through a mix-up in orders the troops on it had retired, and it was held by only a few signalmen. It was one of those moments in war when accident intervenes and offers the palm to either side. The first Confederates up the rocky slopes beheld an enticing sight—Cemetery Ridge, dense with Union troops, an inviting target for artillery fire. At that moment, some Federal units rushed to the hilltop on their own initiative, and more were ordered to follow. Blue and Gray troops clashed savagely in an impromptu, hand-to-hand battle, but at the close of the day the Federals still held Little Round Top. And on Sickles' front the brunt of the Gray assault ground to a stop as darkness fell.

Lee had not cracked the Union line. But he was cheered by the partial success of Longstreet's assault and by the report that Ewell had secured a precarious lodgment on Culp's Hill. One more heavy blow would do it now, he decided. He announced that on the next day he would attack and break the Union center. To this final, climactic endeavor he assigned some 12,000 to 15,000 troops, under the command of George Pickett, a Virginian whose thick curls fell to his shoulders.

On July 3 the Confederates opened in the afternoon with a tremendous bombardment of Cemetery Ridge. For almost two hours the guns fired, while the Federal artillery pulled back to conserve its ammunition for the attack that all knew was coming. At about 3 o'clock the cannonade ceased. On Seminary Ridge, Pickett went to Longstreet and asked: "General, shall I advance?" Longstreet could not bring himself to give the order. He turned in his saddle and looked away. But Pickett understood. He saluted and said, "I am going to move forward, sir."

As the smoke lifted, the Confederate soldiers emerged from the woods on Seminary Ridge and deployed in line of battle. The Union forces watched spellbound. The distance between the two ridges was less than a mile, and the men in gray stood in clear sight of the Federals, as if on a vast stage. One Federal officer wrote in awe: "More than half a mile their front extends; more than a thousand yards the dull gray masses deploy, man touching man, rank pressing rank, and line supporting line. The red flags wave, their horsemen gallop up and down; the arms . . . gleam in the sun, a sloping forest of flashing steel. Right on they move, as with one soul, in perfect order, without impediment of ditch, or wall or stream, over ridge and slope, through orchard and meadow, and cornfield, magnificent, grim, irresistible."

Right on they moved. But they were not irresistible. They were, rather, a great, gleaming target, and after they had covered 200 yards they moved in a sheet of fire. First the artillery shells tore at their ranks and then the rifle fire struck them. The ordered lines wavered and broke, and some units halted or veered off. Fewer than 5,000 men reached the crest of Cemetery Ridge, and these were sucked into the Federal line as into a pocket. As the stunned fragments streamed back to Seminary Ridge, Lee went from group to group offering words of comfort and cheer. He said sadly over and over: "It's all my fault." Perhaps now he realized that it had been hopeless from the beginning.

THE two armies watched each other on July 4, each unaware that on that day Vicksburg was surrendering, and then Lee began to withdraw toward Virginia. Meade followed cautiously. When Lee reached the shore of the Potomac, high water barred his passage, and Meade caught up. It was a magnificent opportunity to smash the Confederate army, but while the Federal general deliberated whether to seize it, the river fell and Lee crossed. Weeks later Meade came to Washington for a conference, and Lincoln could not resist saying to him: "Do you know, general, what your attitude toward Lee for a week after the battle reminded me of?" Meade answered that he did not. "I'll be hanged," said Lincoln, "if I could think of anything else than an old woman trying to shoo her geese across a creek."

Gettysburg was a lustrous opportunity lost and yet also a great victory. On the slopes of Cemetery Ridge the war had taken another of its decisive turns. The total Federal casualties were almost 20,000, but the Confederate figures ran to 25,000. The North could take such losses; the South could not. The Army of Northern Virginia would never be the same again.

General George G. Meade defeated Lee at Gettysburg, but the battle gave him some tense moments. When the two adversaries, who were old acquaintances, met after the war, Lee asked: "What are you doing with all that gray in your beard?" Meade replied wryly: "You have to answer for most of it."

George Edward Pickett, commander of the historic "Pickett's charge," was pre-occupied with his coiffure, which he wore "trimmed and highly perfumed." When a Maryland lady asked General Lee for a lock of hair, he told her he had none to spare but suggested that she ask Pickett. Pickett was not amused.

A lasting record of a tragic time

IN the conflict of the 1860s, for the first time in history, the face of war was recorded in all its ugliness and grandeur by the sharp eye of the camera. Although a few pictures had been taken during the earlier Mexican and Crimean Wars, photography then was limited in scope and quality. Civil War photographers, on the other hand, captured the brutality of battle with shattering impact *(opposite)*, despite the fact that equipment was still unwieldy and the picture-taking process incredibly difficult. The photographer would come careening onto the scene in his lurching wagon, unlimber a camera the size of an orange crate and beg the combatants to freeze in their tracks; then, his picture taken, he would rush into the back of the wagon and develop his glass plates before the images faded forever. The most famous of these harassed cameramen was Mathew B. Brady, a New York photographer who covered the Eastern war from Bull Run to Richmond at his own expense. He hired others to help, and various independents operated in other theaters on their own *(below)*. Among them, these pioneer camera reporters produced an unforgettable history of the war, sometimes shocking but always stirring.

A PHOTOGRAPHER AT WORK, Sam Cooley, with a plate, stops on his way through the South with Sherman to take pictures with his cumbersome camera. He developed plates in a wagon.

A SOLDIER IN DEATH, this young Confederate lies in the Virginia mud, a victim of war's irony. He gave his life on April 2, 1865—seven days before Lee surrendered at Appomattox.

A MORTAR ON TRACKS, the 17,000-pound weapon called "Dictator" squats on its flatcar. When it first fired its 14-pound charge, the resulting shock buckled the undercarriage, which had to be rebuilt.

CANNON ON A FERRY, two guns plus a score of men cross a river aboard a canvas boat designed by the Union's engineers. In 1864 similar boats greatly helped General Sherman's advance on Atlanta.

ENGINEER ON A RAFT, Brigadier General Herman Haupt tests a portable boat designed for scouts. Lincoln called one bridge Haupt designed "the most remarkable structure" he ever saw.

Radical changes in transport caught by the camera

THE camera, itself an innovation in war, recorded many another technological development at an early stage in its growth. Advances in transport, in particular, revolutionized the science of war. Whole armies and mountains of supplies were whisked across country by train; there were men who called Union transportation chief Herman Haupt a genius for his railroad exploits. The tracks also made possible the first railroad guns. Where rail and road transport were difficult, notably in the river-riddled lowlands of the South, Union troops often traveled with their own prefabricated bridges. And the bulky black box of the photographer captured it all.

A BRIDGE ON THE RAPPAHANNOCK easily accommodates a long supply train. The pontoons that supported such bridges were square-ended wooden or canvas boats 20 to 30 feet long; they could be moved overland to an opportune bridge site on carriages. The floats were lashed together with ropes, and the connecting timbers were often hewn from the adjacent forests.

The tools of destruction

The tremendous weight of Northern production is illustrated repeatedly in Civil War photographs, and never more effectively than in this picture of Union artillery drawn up in long rows on the wharves of Yorktown, Virginia, near the site of the final siege of the Revolution 81 years earlier. Photographed

during the first great Federal drive in the East—McClellan's Peninsular Campaign against Richmond in the spring of 1862 —these weapons were the first trickle of a vast flood of war manufactures that would ultimately overwhelm the South. Along the shore at the right are rows of cast-iron, muzzle-load-ing Parrott artillery pieces. In the foreground are little Coe-horn mortars; they were short-ranged but accurate, and were light enough for men to carry. Mortars were used extensively in the war and accounted for heavy casualties—though the troops learned to spot the shells in flight and dash for cover.

For the wounded,
the painful sequel of battle

ALTHOUGH the photography of the period was too clumsy to permit action shots, the consequences of battle were depicted in hundreds of pictures. The story they tell is not a pleasant one. Medicine was crude—and Civil War wounds would have taxed the skill of a modern surgeon. The soft bullets of the period—called Minié balls after their French inventor—ranged up to .69 of an inch in diameter, an enormous size for a bullet, and they struck with mutilating force. The wounded often waited a day or longer before taking a jolting ambulance ride to the hospital. There, a set of doors often served as an operating table, and the usual treatment was "radical surgery"—the standard euphemism for amputation.

MAKE-BELIEVE WOUNDED are loaded into an ambulance as corpsmen practice their job. After a battle, wounded were collected in any available wagon—often one without springs.

UNION WOUNDED from the Wilderness in 1864 sun themselves outside a field hospital, probably a commandeered building, near Fredericksburg, Virginia. A nurse sits in the doorway.

CONFEDERATE WOUNDED, attended by a Union doctor, lie under improvised shelters after Antietam in September 1862. Earlier, both sides had classed surgeons as noncombatants.

NORTHERN PRISONERS at Andersonville muster under the blistering Georgia sun to receive their pittance of food. Everything was so scarce a man with a frying pan could get a portion of his messmates' rations merely for supplying the pot to cook it in. After the war, a public outcry arose over Andersonville; the commander, Major Henry Wirz, was tried and executed.

The grinding misery of the prisoner of war

For the Civil War soldier there was one fate that was worse than being wounded, and almost worse than death itself. That was to be captured. Prisoners on both sides died by the thousands, victims of disease, starvation, exposure and neglect. At the infamous Confederate prison, Andersonville, there was a period when one Northerner died every 11 minutes. Southerners in Northern prisons suffered cruelly from the cold. There was some excuse for the appalling conditions in the hard-hit South, but in the rich North prison conditions were often the result of sheer negligence. In all, death claimed more than 26,000 Southerners of the 220,000 held prisoner; the toll among Northerners was 22,500 out of 127,000—a lower figure but a higher percentage. Yet strangely, neither Northern nor Southern officials seemed ashamed of the terrible conditions in the camps; cameramen were permitted to photograph them freely.

SOUTHERN PRISONERS lounge outside their barracks at Elmira, New York. This was a neater camp than Andersonville—but in one period some 2,000 of its 8,000 captives were sick or dying.

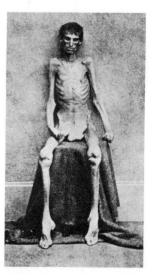

A SURVIVOR looks like a skeleton after his liberation from Andersonville. More than one prisoner out of every three held at Andersonville died.

THE DEAD at Andersonville are consigned to a common trench grave by fellow prisoners. Burials were swift, to reduce the spread of disease.

75

A HARD CHOICE confronts Grant as he studies a map over General Meade's shoulder. Grant rarely consulted subordinates; he made this decision, like most others, himself.

Historic photographs of a critical decision

In 1864 General U. S. Grant hammered at the Confederates with crushing blows. In June the Southerners entrenched at Cold Harbor, Virginia, and Grant had to decide whether to attack their strong position. As he reached his decision at his improvised headquarters—the front lawn of nearby Bethesda Church—a photographer, Timothy O'Sullivan, went to the steeple and took these pictures. At left, Grant, seated in a pew in front of the trees, writes the order for the attack. The wagons and ambulances on the road beyond would soon be busy: the battle, a failure, cost him 12,700 men.

77

Professionals at the art of war

By 1864 the raw recruits of the early days—dry goods clerks, farm boys, city wastrels—had become the steady, battle-tested professional soldiers shown here. But there was by now a qualitative difference between the Northern fighting man and his Confederate foe. The Rebels were growing increasingly hag-

gard and hungry; the Federals were better equipped, better fed, better commanded and in better health than at any time since the war began. Surprisingly, Union officers found that the scrawny city youths of 1861 had fared better than their burly country cousins; somehow the farmers, accustomed to an unvarying routine as civilians, found it hard to adjust to the irregularity of soldier life. Nevertheless, the time came when photographers were able to produce evidence like this picture to prove to the people back home, in Northern city and village alike, that their menfolk at the front were ready for anything.

79

4. THE WAR'S FINAL AGONY

VICKSBURG and the Mississippi in Union hands, the striking power of Robert E. Lee's army blunted beyond repair and, in Tennessee, the Federal troops of W. S. Rosecrans poised to move against Confederate Chattanooga—all these momentous events coming to a climax in the first week of July 1863 presaged disaster for the Confederacy. Inexorably the balance was swinging against the South.

But the deadly shift could still be halted. If the Confederates could hold Chattanooga and the Tennessee River line, they might be able to mount an offensive that would restore in part the situation in the West.

Rosecrans spent the first part of the summer strengthening his army and writing long, angry letters to Washington charging that he was not properly supported or appreciated. When at last he advanced toward Chattanooga in late August, he was still bursting with irritation, and he seemed to be laboring under great inner tension. But he moved with his usual skill in maneuver. As he approached Chattanooga, Bragg evacuated the city, a potential trap; the Confederate general wanted room in which to fight. Rosecrans pushed after him, finally taking up a position behind the little stream of Chickamauga, an Indian name meaning "river of death." Bragg was determined to attack. Reinforcements—Longstreet and most of his corps—were on the way from the stalemated Virginia front, but Bragg did not wait. On September 19, when only three brigades of Longstreet's men had arrived, he ordered an attack. At

PRODUCING FOR WAR, a Union foundry casts molten ore for cannon. By 1864 the vast quantities of weapons pouring from Northern factories were overwhelming the South.

the end of the day he had gained no advantage, but that night the rest of Longstreet's troops arrived. The Confederates now had what was rare for them, a numerical advantage—some 70,000 to 56,000.

On the 20th Bragg resumed the offensive all along the line. As the two armies slugged away at each other in fierce fighting, another of those dramatic accidents of war intervened to alter the face of the battle. It was reported to Rosecrans, incorrectly, that one of his divisions on the right was not properly supported. Without checking, he excitedly pulled another division out of the line to close up on the one threatened. Longstreet, probing at the Union right, found a large gap in the line. He poured his men through in a smashing surge.

More than the physical collapse of an army wing occurred at that moment. Rosecrans, in the crisis of his career, gave way to those tensions and doubts that had always been with him. He and two of his corps generals left the field and rode in frantic haste to Chattanooga.

What made his flight look so bad was that the battle continued. His left, under the stubborn George H. Thomas, remained on the field, holding off the whole Confederate army. For his stand that day Thomas was known ever after as the "Rock of Chickamauga." He could not, however, fight indefinitely. At nightfall, under orders from Rosecrans, he retired. By the next day the entire Army of the Cumberland lay huddled in the Chattanooga defenses.

CHICKAMAUGA was one of the bloodiest battles of the war. Confederate casualties were an appalling 25 per cent. Because of his losses and his natural irresolution, Bragg was slow to exploit his victory. But he finally occupied Missionary Ridge, Lookout Mountain and other heights south of Chattanooga. Mounting artillery at advantageous points, he could command the supply routes leading into the city, and he laid it under a modified siege. Soon the Federal army ran dangerously short of supplies.

In this crisis of Federal arms, Lincoln named Grant commander of all armies in the Western theater. Immediately Grant relieved Rosecrans and replaced him with Thomas. Then Grant went to Chattanooga to see for himself the condition of affairs.

He found them brightening. The high command had sent in from the Eastern army 20,000 men, who had been transported by rail 1,200 miles in 14 days, the most dramatic feat of its kind in the war. And the supply route had been partially opened, and some goods were coming in. Characteristically Grant prepared to take the offensive. As a first step, he ordered part of his own Army of the Tennessee brought to Chattanooga.

While the Federal camps hummed with activity, dissension occupied Bragg and his generals. Some of the commanders were critical of Bragg's conduct in the battle, and he blamed some of them for the failure to achieve a greater success. The quarrel became so bitter that President Davis had to journey to Bragg's headquarters to try to mediate it. At a painful conference Davis asked the corps generals in Bragg's presence to state their opinion of their commander. Each one said in effect that Bragg lacked the competence to lead.

Surprisingly, after all this Davis retained Bragg in command. The President gave as his reason that he could not find an adequate successor. There was one available, Joe Johnston, but Davis distrusted and detested him. Another curious result followed this strange episode. Longstreet had spoken strongly against Bragg, and he was obviously unhappy at serving under him. At Davis'

General James Longstreet, one of Robert E. Lee's most able corps commanders, became a successful New Orleans insurance and cotton broker after the war, but incurred Southern wrath by turning Republican. From 1869 to 1904 he held a series of federal offices, including that of minister to Turkey.

Winning or losing, Confederate General Braxton Bragg lacked confidence in himself. Victorious at Chickamauga, he went to bed refusing to believe he had won. Routed at Chattanooga, he criticized himself without mercy. "The disaster," he wrote, "is justly disparaging to me as a commander."

suggestion and with Bragg's approval, "Old Pete" was sent off on a foolish expedition against Knoxville, bringing Bragg's army down to well under 50,000.

By late November Grant was ready to strike. He now had a force of 60,000 men. He first sent a column to occupy Lookout Mountain on the Confederate left. The Federals went up the rugged sides in a heavy mist that hid them from the sight of the watchers below. The attackers won the position against light opposition. The Confederates, expecting an assault, had withdrawn most of their troops to what they considered the key to their line: Missionary Ridge, farther to the right. On the 25th the Federal army flung its full strength against this steep 600-foot height.

Grant's plan was to hold the attention of the Confederates in his front with Thomas' Army of the Cumberland, while his own Army of the Tennessee under W. T. Sherman won the battle by crushing the Rebel right. It did not work out at all as Grant planned. In fact, Missionary Ridge became an unplanned battle, directed largely by the common soldiers. Sherman found the going so rough that he had to call on Grant for help. Grant directed Thomas to send his men against the first line of enemy rifle pits at the foot of the ridge, then halt and await further orders. Halfway up was another line and then the main Rebel position on the crest.

The officers and men of the Army of the Cumberland either did not understand the order or chose to ignore it. They had been through the carnage of Chickamauga, and they had taken some cruel taunts from Grant's men, the cocky victors of Vicksburg. Now they were determined to show what they were made of. They swept through the first line of rifle pits and then, as if animated by a sudden mass will, they charged up the heights. A fighting frenzy drove them now. At the same time some counteremotion of despair or panic gripped the Confederates. They gave way precipitately. So rapid was the Federal advance and so sudden the Confederate collapse that both lines seemed to go over the crest together. Bragg vainly tried to rally his fleeing men. "Here's your commander," he cried. "Here's your jackass," they answered and continued on their way. Bragg had to retire to Dalton, Georgia, and from there he asked to be relieved. Davis reluctantly granted the request and with even more reluctance gave the command to Johnston.

The Federals now proceeded to occupy most of eastern Tennessee. They had achieved the second of their great strategic objectives—the possession of Chattanooga and the Tennessee line. It was the third turning point of the war. If the Confederates had held the Tennessee line, they could possibly have launched another offensive. Now they no longer possessed the capacity to win independence by a military decision. They could only hope to exhaust the Northern will to fight.

As the fateful year of 1864 opened, all the advantages were with the Union. Northern manpower and industry were reaching peak strength, while Southern resources were running out. The blockade was achieving an ever-tighter effectiveness. In August the navy would occupy the harbor of Mobile, leaving only Wilmington and Charleston operating, though much reduced.

Most important of all, Northern land forces were now co-ordinated. Ulysses S. Grant had assumed command of all Union armies, and his plan was to press against the Rebels everywhere at once; those troops not fighting, he told Lincoln, could aid the fighting by advancing. Yes, replied Lincoln, he

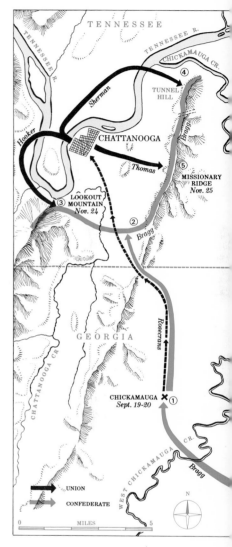

BREAKING THE SIEGE
OF CHATTANOOGA

Toward the end of 1863, General Bragg's Rebels attacked Rosecrans at Chickamauga (1) and won a smashing victory. Union forces, knocked back into Chattanooga, were besieged by Bragg (2). At this point Grant took over—and ordered an attack. Hooker seized Lookout Mountain (3) on the Confederate left, but Sherman ran into trouble on the right (4). Thomas' men, ordered to divert Bragg in the center, instead smashed straight up Missionary Ridge (5) and broke the Confederate line. This opened the way for Sherman's advance on Atlanta and his march to the sea.

understood the principle; and he uttered a military maxim that many West Pointers would not have grasped but that Grant, coming from much the same rural background, caught: "Those not skinning can hold a leg," said the Commander in Chief. A simultaneous offensive was the strategy that Lincoln had vainly proposed to all his previous generals.

Grant's plan called for three major offensives. In the Eastern theater the Army of the Potomac would take Lee's army, the most formidable Confederate force, as its objective instead of Richmond. The Army of the Potomac technically continued under Meade's command. But Grant accompanied it and actually directed its operations. His instructions to Meade had an iron simplicity: "Wherever Lee goes, there you will go also."

There were to be two coinciding offensives in the West. At Chattanooga Sherman commanded the armies that had defeated Bragg. This combined force of 100,000 was to move into northern Georgia, destroy the Confederate army under Johnston and seize the industrial center of Atlanta. At the same time the Federal army under N. P. Banks in New Orleans would advance to Mobile and then possibly to Montgomery, where it could co-operate with Sherman.

Banks's part in the triple offensive never came off. In March, six weeks before the big jump-off was scheduled, he embarked on an expedition northwestward, up the Red River, to occupy Shreveport and possibly enter Texas. Another Federal army was to advance south from Arkansas. The two forces expected to squeeze between them the Confederates under Kirby Smith, commanding in the Trans-Mississippi theater. Banks moved ahead briskly and with hardly any security precautions. Below Shreveport his army was strung out in a loose march formation. Suddenly a smaller Confederate force under Richard Taylor hit him near Mansfield, shearing through the extended Federals like a huge knife. Banks retired to Pleasant Hill, where on the next day he held Taylor off in a sharp fight. Banks might have resumed his advance now, but he was too shaken. He retreated to New Orleans, while the Federals from Arkansas also fell back. The long march had so exhausted Banks's army that it could not take its part in Grant's plan.

A young "powder monkey" leans against a cannon on board the U.S.S. "New Hampshire." Thousands of youngsters served both sides in the Civil War; a number of Union soldiers were less than 15 years old. The North boasted one 20-year-old general, Galusha Pennypacker, and there is a story, perhaps apocryphal, that the Confederacy had a 13-year-old captain.

Both Grant and Sherman pushed off in the first week of May. The Army of the Potomac, 120,000 strong, plunged into the desolate Wilderness, where just a year before Hooker had met disaster. Grant hoped to bring Lee to a showdown battle and end the war at one stroke. His plan was to move by his left and seek to envelop Lee's right, holding his rival and forcing him to fight. He was quietly confident, but his generals were not. Grant still had to convince his own army that Lee was not the greatest commander of the war.

Grant hoped to get through the Wilderness before meeting Lee and to fight the decisive battle in open country. But Lee boldly placed his own army in the Wilderness squarely astride the path of the Federals. In the dense thickets which favored the defenders he hoped to throw Grant back and annihilate him as he had almost done to Hooker. Grant accepted the challenge.

The battle of the Wilderness began on May 5. The fighting was savage and confused. Grant attacked and smashed Lee's right. But at the critical moment fresh troops from Longstreet's corps, now back under Lee, launched a damaging counterattack. At the end of two days Grant had not been able to envelop Lee or to force a showdown. Both sides had suffered frightful casualties, and many of the wounded, trapped in woods set afire by artillery shells, burned to death horribly.

After the battle Grant disappeared from Lee's front. The old, weary pattern for the North seemed about to repeat itself. A Federal general had been defeated by Lee; now he would retire to reorganize and come on again in a month or so. Possibly Lee thought it would be this way. Grant's own army was sure it would be so. The tired men were trudging eastward on the night of May 7. Suddenly in the dark woods the column turned to the south, instead of to the north and safety. At the same time Grant rode by. These were veteran soldiers, and they knew the meaning of a movement. They were not going back after all, but forward, forward to Richmond. Exhausted and sore as they were, they still rushed to the roadside to cheer Grant, to shout in sheer exultation. Grant was heading to his left and toward Spotsylvania. It was the supreme movement of the campaign. Right then Grant had won the game as surely as if he had crushed the Confederate army. He still had a long road ahead before the formal ending. But he had done what no other Federal general had been able to do—he had refused to let Lee impose his will on him.

Lee shifted to meet Grant, and at Spotsylvania on May 9 through 12 the armies fought another bloody engagement. Employing superb engineering skill, Lee constructed field fortifications in the form of a salient. Grant threw his men against these works in waves. Here at the "Bloody Angle" the lines stood within 50 feet of each other and blazed away for hours. Bodies were shot to pieces—one was found with 80 bullets in it. So thick was the small-arms fire that an oak tree 23 inches in diameter was shredded to fiber six feet from the ground; it blew down that night. The Confederates, badly shaken, still hung on to their position. Losses on both sides were again heavy.

Undaunted, Grant again sidled off to his left—and, when Lee occupied a position too strong for the Federals to attack, to his left again. Lee kept pace. By the first of June the two armies had reached Cold Harbor, northeast of Richmond. Here Grant made a last attempt to force a decision in open country. In one fierce frontal assault he lost 7,000 men. Now he had to pause to consider his next move. The first phase of the campaign was ended.

For a month the contending armies had fought almost every day. Nothing like this sustained and savage fighting had been seen before in the war. Grant had lost in total casualties 55,000 men, but with replacements his army stood at its original size. Lee had started the campaign with 65,000 troops. His losses were 32,000, and he would have to scrape the barrel to replenish his ranks. Grant's constant slugging was slowly sapping Confederate strength.

DURING the struggle at Spotsylvania, Grant had informed his government that he would never turn back. "I . . . purpose to fight it out on this line if it takes all summer," he wrote. But now he had to adjust his strategy. If he continued to maneuver on his present line, Lee would retire into the Richmond defenses and invite a long and costly siege. Grant decided to make one more attempt to bring his wily foe to battle, this time below Richmond.

On the night of June 12, he disappeared once more from Lee's front. He was making for Petersburg, 23 miles south of Richmond and the hub of the railroads serving the capital. If he could seize Petersburg, he would stand on the life lines that fed Richmond and the Confederate army, and Lee would have to come out and fight for his communications. It was a daring move—just the

Union Admiral John A. Dahlgren, who spent 16 years at the Bureau of Ordnance, was the inventor of the "Dahlgren gun." This naval cannon, which was called a "soda-bottle gun" because a narrow barrel and thick breech gave it the look of a cast-iron flagon, proved so effective in sea battles that one naval historian has called it the weapon that won the Civil War.

kind Lee himself would have made—and for five days it deceived Lee. When the Army of the Potomac arrived before Petersburg, it found only 14,000 men under General Beauregard protecting the approaches to Richmond. Once again it seemed that Grant had victory in his grasp.

Again the prize was snatched away. Beauregard put up a superb fight and, bluffing magnificently, gave the impression that he was much stronger than he was. For three days he held off all attacks. He was helped by the Federal generals on the spot, who delivered their assaults in piecemeal fashion. But finally the sheer arithmetic of the situation asserted itself. On the night of June 17 Beauregard's tired men knew that they could not withstand another onslaught. At 7:30 the next morning as they braced themselves for a last effort, they saw Lee's troops arriving and filing into the works. Lee had at last accepted Grant's presence at Petersburg and moved rapidly to the threatened point. Petersburg and Richmond had been saved.

Now Grant realized that he could not win a quick victory. Lee's army was behind field fortifications and would not come out. Grant could get at Lee only by capturing Petersburg, and this could be accomplished only by the slow method of siege. Both armies dug in. The Confederate line stretched for about 50 miles from above Richmond to below Petersburg, and the Federal trenches paralleled it. Constantly Grant sought to extend his line and his troops to the left to get on the precious railroads.

Lee had but one hope. If he could force Grant to detach strength to another theater, then possibly he could drive the main Federal army back. It was a desperate gamble, but Lee was willing to take it. He strengthened his force in the Valley under Jubal Early and ordered Early to threaten Washington. Early was no Jackson, and the Valley army of 1864 was not the dashing column of the exuberant days of 1862. But Early did his best. He slashed northward and raided the outskirts of the Federal capital. But he did not have the strength to drive his threat home. The defensive forces around Washington, aided by some troops from Grant's army, compelled him to retire.

At Lincoln's urging Grant acted to remove the menace of Early permanently. All the Washington defense forces were placed under the command of Grant's cavalry leader, Philip Sheridan, an aggressive five-foot-five-inch bantam of a man. Sheridan's instructions were to smash Early so completely that the Federals would never have to worry again about the Valley route to Washington. Sheridan did the job thoroughly in the autumn, in the battles of Winchester, Fisher's Hill and Cedar Creek. Lee's plan had failed. The siege of Petersburg went on. It would endure for more than nine bitter months.

In that same first week in May when Grant plunged into the Wilderness, Sherman moved forward from Chattanooga, toward Joe Johnston's army and, beyond Johnston, booming, industrial Atlanta. The campaign pitted two masters of maneuver against each other. Sherman advanced and sought to envelop Johnston. Johnston slipped back and avoided the trap. Only at one place, Kennesaw Mountain, did a real battle occur, and it was indecisive.

In this leapfrog fashion the two armies went back almost to Atlanta itself. Johnston's failure to stop Sherman disgusted Davis. The Confederate President had never liked the general, and now he removed him and appointed John B. Hood, one of the corps officers, to the command. A blond giant, Hood had been a superb unit leader. But he did not possess the capacity for army

To retaliate for Sheridan's laying waste of the Shenandoah Valley (opposite), some 20 to 25 Confederates slipped across the Canadian border and raided St. Albans, Vermont. They held up three banks, forced a teller to swear allegiance to the Confederacy (above), collected $200,000 and headed back to Canada, burning the bridge at Sheldon (below) to prevent pursuit.

command. Nor was his wracked physical condition—an arm mangled and a leg lost in battle—conducive to mental sharpness.

When a Federal officer who had known Hood in Texas before the war heard of the appointment, he predicted an immediate battle. He had played poker with Hood, he explained, and "a man who will bet a thousand dollars without having a pair in his hand will fight when he has the troops with which to do it." The analysis was accurate. Hood immediately delivered two consecutive fierce attacks on Sherman's approaching columns.

When these failed to check the Federals, Hood retired into Atlanta with the idea of forcing Sherman to resort to a siege. Sherman for a time did employ siege methods. But he had no mind to be held up very long. A lone railroad line from the south served the city, and Sherman seized it in a quick wheeling movement, forcing Hood to evacuate. Over the wires to Washington on September 3 went a singing message from Sherman: "So Atlanta is ours, and fairly won." The victory helped to return Lincoln to the White House in the election nine weeks later.

S HERMAN had Atlanta, but he had not executed the most vital part of his assignment, which had been to destroy the enemy army. Indeed, Hood now proceeded to recover in part the initiative. Moving northwest, he struck Sherman's railroad communications above Atlanta in a series of hit-and-run raids. Sherman chased him but in a halfhearted way. The Federal commander did not believe he could bring Hood to bay and had little interest in doing so.

Sherman had fixed his mind on a new plan of operations; on, in fact, a new concept of war. Tall and red-haired, a concentrated bundle of nervous energy, Sherman had the most modern mind of the Civil War generals. He was far from being a great combat soldier, but he had grasped one of the great principles that would distinguish the conflicts of the future. The will of an enemy nation to resist rested on the people sheltered behind the armies. Sherman proposed now to bring the war home to the civilian population of the South.

He broached his plan to Grant. He would send back to Tennessee 30,000 men under Thomas. This force with other troops that Thomas could collect should be enough to hold the Tennessee line against Hood or any other Confederate invader. Then, after wrecking Atlanta so that the Rebels could not return to use it as a base, Sherman with 62,000 men would swing across Georgia, destroying economic resources as he went. He would come out at some point on the coast where the navy would open up a base for him; from there he could march to join Grant before Richmond. The plan held out great possibilities and also great risks. If anything should go wrong in Sherman's rear, he would have to retrace his steps. Grant gave his assent with some hesitation.

By a dramatic coincidence, Hood at the same time decided on a plan to invade Tennessee. Sherman would have to follow him, Hood reasoned, and in the mountains he could turn and defeat the pursuers. Radiant hopes flashed before him as he considered the possibilities. With Sherman smashed, the Confederate army could drive on to the Ohio River. Or it could march eastward to join Lee and destroy Grant before Richmond.

If Sherman's scheme was risky, Hood's bordered on the fantastic. The Confederate was going to save his cause by pulling out a last great victory—and he was going to do it all with only a little more than 40,000 men. Oddly enough, he might have succeeded in part; if he had advanced quickly enough,

In October 1864, Confederates attacked General Philip Sheridan's troops at Cedar Creek, Virginia. "Sheridan, 20 miles away," as a famous poem has it, spurred to the front and rallied his men. He then continued the ruthless sacking of the Shenandoah Valley so Rebel forces could not use it again. When one of his men was shot he had all houses within five miles razed.

he might have forced Sherman to return. But having conceived an audacious plan, Hood hesitated to execute it. When he finally moved, it was too late.

Even so, when he entered Tennessee the only organized force opposing him consisted of 30,000 troops under General Schofield. This force tried to delay Hood, but he caught up with it on November 30 at Franklin, just south of Nashville, and ordered an attack. An air of doom seemed to hang over the Confederates. Both officers and men had been enraged at Hood's remarks that the army had retreated so long under Johnston that it had forgotten how to attack. Now they would show him regardless of the costs.

The charge of Hood's men at Franklin was one of the great assaults of the war, fully as dramatic as Pickett's dash at Gettysburg. To reach the strong Federal position, the Confederates had to attack across two miles of open space swept by fire. Six times they flung themselves forward and each time recoiled. Over 6,000 Rebels fell and 11 generals were killed or wounded. As cold darkness closed on the field, the Federals retired intact to Nashville. All of Hood's bright dreams had crashed. But he could not admit failure. He moved his army forward and occupied a dismal winter line south of Nashville.

In the city Thomas was preparing to attack. "Old Pap" Thomas was one of the most unappreciated generals of the war. He was deliberate and meticulous, and when he finally acted the result was devastating. He was putting together a force for what he meant to be an irresistible blow. He would have, when he was finished, an army of 57,000 men, including the most formidable cavalry aggregation of the war: 12,000 troopers under James H. Wilson.

On December 15 Thomas came out and attacked Hood. His infantry smashed at the Confederate front while his cavalry rode rapidly to envelop and turn the Gray left. Driven from the field on the first day, Hood attempted to set up another line on the second. Thomas crushed it ruthlessly, and the Rebel remnants broke and fled. Even then Thomas did not relax his pressure. Union cavalry harried the retreating Confederates for 26 days and 200 miles. No other army in the war was subjected to such a pursuit. Not until Hood reached northern Mississippi was he safe. Every general on both sides dreamed of winning a victory so complete that the enemy army ceased to exist. Thomas came the closest. The Confederate Army of Tennessee was no longer a fighting force, and Sherman would not have to return to deal with a threat in his rear.

ON November 15 Sherman and his 62,000 troopers swung out from burning Atlanta. They were beginning the great march of the war, the march to the sea. Sherman in his correspondence often referred to the operation as a "raid," and accurately so. This was a raid on a gigantic scale, not against the communications of an enemy army but against the economic resources of an enemy civilian population. It was modern war, swift, terrible and merciless.

The Blue army moved virtually unopposed, marching on a 60-mile front. Its wagon trains carried only the most essential of supplies. Before Sherman lay the fat farm lands of Georgia, bursting with foods after the harvest, and he intended to subsist on the country. His orders were to "forage liberally."

The foragers, also known as "bummers" and "smokehouse rangers," indulged in the loosest interpretation of Sherman's instructions concerning the destruction of property. Technically, by these orders only resources potentially useful to the enemy were to be razed or appropriated—factories, railroads, cotton gins, surplus supplies. But the whole army knew that Sher-

When General George H. Thomas of Virginia sided with the Union, his relatives cried that he should change his name, and his picture was turned to the wall in their Virginia estate. But when Thomas held the line at Chickamauga, one Rebel general proudly noted it was an "indomitable Virginia soldier . . . who saved the Union army from total rout and ruin."

man wanted to humble the South, and it was ready to help him. An invading army in any war is convinced that enemy civilians are fair prey, and this army was encouraged by the known views of its commander. The soldiers did not have to be told that Sherman would be understanding in enforcing discipline. The bummers stole and burned, sometimes in a mood of vengeance but usually in a spirit of horseplay that was even more infuriating to Southerners. Georgians raged when they heard that laughing Blue soldiers at the state capital had confiscated stacks of bank notes to make fires for their coffee.

A picnic air characterized the whole march. Hordes of blacks attached themselves to the columns, some 25,000 at one time or another, to find out what freedom was, to be a part of the fun, to offer their services in menial and military capacities. Most of these were turned back—they impeded the march —but 6,800 went on to the sea. At the end of a day's trek, huge fires of pine knots lit up the camps while the men rested, played cards, listened to the bands send out their melodies to the mournful woods and sang bellowing songs. Southerners would remember the march through Georgia with bitterness and hatred. Sherman's men would recall only the pleasures.

By late December Sherman was on the coast at Savannah, announcing in a dramatic telegram to Lincoln that he was presenting the city to him as a Christmas present. From there he headed north to join Grant. Into South Carolina he rolled, dealing out more retribution to that most-Southern state

**TWO-PRONGED STRATEGY
THAT ENDED THE WAR**

In the closing months of the war, Federals caught the Confederates between two vast pincers. In Virginia, Grant, in a series of battles, drove Lee into Richmond-Petersburg (1) and besieged him. At last, his defenses broken at Five Forks, Lee fled, surrendering at Appomattox. In the west, Sherman advanced from Chattanooga (2) to take Atlanta (3). Then, despite Hood's attempt to draw him off into Tennessee (4) he swept across Georgia to the sea (5) and then northward through the Carolinas. Five days after Appomattox he accepted Johnston's surrender at Durham (6).

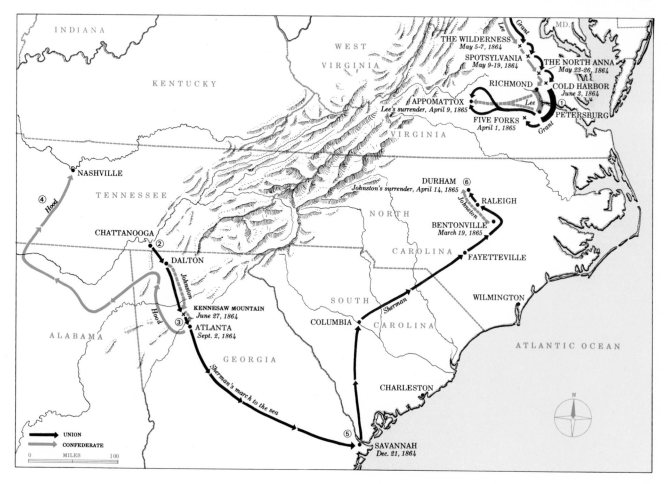

than to Georgia, and then into North Carolina. The Confederate government finally collected an army of 30,000 to oppose him and called on Joe Johnston to command it. But he could do little more than delay Sherman's advance.

Sherman had destroyed uncalculated amounts of Southern property. But the greatest effect of his march, as he intended, was psychological. The spectacle of a Federal army flowing unimpeded through the heart of the Confederacy was a harbinger that not even the stoutest Southerner could ignore.

Captain James I. Waddell of the famous Rebel cruiser "Shenandoah" is depicted in a cartoon as Rip Van Winkle, learning in 1865 that the Civil War has been over for some months. During its 13-month cruise the Confederate raider traveled all the way around the world and destroyed more than $1.3 million worth of Yankee shipping— much of it after the war had ended.

B UT Sherman's accomplishment, sensational as it was, could not in itself bring the Confederacy down. The end would not come until the principal Confederate force left in the field, Lee's army, was destroyed. And only Grant possessed the will to deliver the death blow. For long weary months he had pounded at Petersburg without effect. Then suddenly, in the first week of April 1865, he broke through. He passed a force around the Confederate right and at Five Forks rolled up the enemy flank. The whole Confederate line collapsed. Lee fell back, and the Federals marched into Petersburg and—at a proud moment—through Richmond.

It was almost finished now. The Army of Northern Virginia, shrunken by deaths and desertions to 25,000 men, crawled westward. Lee nourished a flickering hope that he might be able to reach a rail line to North Carolina and unite with Johnston. But the pursuing Federals moved faster and closed off his escape route. The great Confederate realized at last that continued resistance was hopeless. With anguished heart but knowing his duty, he determined to surrender his army. He wrote to Grant to ask for a meeting, and Grant, also anxious to end the useless fighting, accepted. They met on April 9, Palm Sunday, in the little village of Appomattox Courthouse in the house of a man named Wilmer McLean. McLean had owned the farm on Bull Run where the first great battle of the war occurred. He had moved from such a dangerous area, and now at the last the war had caught up with him again.

Lee came to the meeting accompanied by one staff officer and formally attired: a gleaming, splendid martial figure. Grant came in from the line, a dozen generals and staff officers following him, and wearing his customary careless dress. There was a symbolism in the confrontation—Lee the knightly soldier, the representative of a way of war and of life that was disappearing, and Grant, the businessman in uniform, the exponent of future war.

After some casual conversation, Grant, at Lee's request, sat down to write his terms. They were generously simple. The officers and men of the Army of Northern Virginia were to sign paroles that they would fight no more, and then they could go home. There would have to be a ceremonial stacking of weapons, although officers could retain their sidearms and horses.

Lee read the document carefully. He was moved and said: "This will have a very happy effect on my army." After a slight hesitation he remarked that many of his soldiers owned their own mounts; "I would like to understand whether these men will be permitted to retain their horses." The Federal general reflected a moment and said: "I will not change the terms as now written, but I will instruct the officers I shall appoint to receive the paroles to let all the men who claim to own a horse or mule take the animals home with them to work their little farms." Lee, much affected, replied: "This will have the best possible effect upon the men. It will be very gratifying and will do much toward conciliating our people."

Drafts of the terms were now drawn up for the two generals to sign. A brief conversation followed, and then Lee took his departure. He came onto the porch and called for his horse. While he waited, he thrice smote his right fist into the left palm as if in inner agony. As he mounted, Grant came out. He raised his hat in salute. Lee returned the gesture and rode off to tell his men that they would have to surrender.

The formal surrender came on April 12. To receive it Grant designated General Joshua Chamberlain, a former college professor turned good soldier and a man of delicate perceptions. Chamberlain saw the Confederates on the opposite slopes breaking their last camp, saw them march forward at their famous route step, their battle flags waving so thickly above the thinned ranks that the column "seemed crowned with red." He resolved to mark the occasion with a proper gesture, and he offered no excuse for his decision. As he explained it later: "Before us in proud humiliation stood the embodiment of manhood: men whom neither toils and sufferings, nor the fact of death, nor disaster, nor hopelessness could bend from their resolve; standing before us now, thin, worn, and famished, but erect, and with eyes looking level into ours, waking memories that bound us together as no other bond;—was not such manhood to be welcomed back into a Union so tested and assured?"

When the sad Gray column reached Chamberlain's line, a signal sounded. Instantly the Blue ranks shifted from "order arms" to the "marching salute," the highest honor fighting men could give to other fighting men. Riding at the head of the Confederate marchers with downcast face was General John B. Gordon, a magnificent figure of a man on a magnificent horse. Gordon heard the slapping of Federal hands on muskets, caught the meaning of the gesture and, wheeling his horse upright, dropped the point of his sword and ordered his men to return the salute. It was a moment of solemn splendor, and Chamberlain recorded it in moving words: "On our part not a sound of trumpet more, nor roll of drum; not a cheer, nor word nor whisper of vainglorying, nor motion of man standing again at the order, but an awed stillness rather, and breath-holding, as if it were the passing of the dead!"

Slowly the tidings that Lee had surrendered spread to all parts of the Confederacy. All knew now that the end had come. All but Jefferson Davis—the tortured President fled Richmond, still believing that somehow, somewhere he could yet arouse his people to fight on. He was captured by Federal cavalry in Georgia. Joe Johnston surrendered to Sherman near Durham, North Carolina, and then one by one other Rebel generals in Alabama, Mississippi and Louisiana laid down their arms. By June 1 all organized resistance had ceased.

IT was all over now, the ordeal of the Union, the great crimson gash in American history. It was finished but the names would never die. They would live on and would stir men's minds even in later generations—Bull Run, Shiloh Church, The Seven Days, Antietam Creek, Cemetery Ridge, Chickamauga, Appomattox. And something else had ended with the last guns: the old Union, that Union of states and sections and of a distant and aloof national government. It was gone forever, sunk in the receding past. An American nation had emerged out of the blazing test of civil war. It was a nation that would have to meet many problems, some of them developing out of the war itself and some of them new and strangely complex. But henceforth it would act in every crisis as a great central power.

General Robert E. Lee rides back toward his lines after Appomattox. Advising Southerners to put aside "thoughts of the past and fears of the future," he became president of Washington College in Lexington, Virginia, though it had only 50 students. Before long it was known as "General Lee's College"; after his death it was renamed "Washington and Lee."

At Shiloh, raw troops clash in a massive pitched battle in April 1862. The Rebels were winning until they stopped to plunder enemy tents.

A fearsome pageant of destruction

ONLY in retrospect, after the Civil War ended, could the combatants begin to grasp the scope of the mighty conflict. It had been a far cry from the one-strike triumph both North and South had expected before the bloody Union rout at First Bull Run *(opposite)*. It had turned into a vast, grinding war of attrition in which one critical battle followed hard on the heels of the last *(next pages)*. Not until the summer of 1864 was there a real break in the deadly equilibrium between the South's superior generalship and the North's preponderant manpower; and even after Lincoln found in Grant a match for Lee, bitter fighting dragged on for months.

In the end, no single feature of the war stood out more sharply than the courage of the ordinary soldier on both sides. It is no wonder that Union General Joshua Chamberlain, accepting the surrender of his enemies at Appomattox, found himself deeply moved. "What visions thronged as we looked into each other's eyes," he wrote. "Here pass the men of Antietam, the . . . survivors of the terrible Wilderness . . . Cobb's Georgia Legion, which held the stone wall on Marye's Heights. . . . Now the sad great pageant—Longstreet and his men. . . . Ah, is this Pickett's Division?—this little group left of those who on the lurid last day of Gettysburg breasted level cross-fire and thunderbolts of storm, to be strewn back drifting wrecks. . . . How could we help falling on our knees, all of us together, and praying God to pity and forgive us all!"

AT FIRST BULL RUN, General Barnard Bee (*mounted, foreground*) rallies his faltering Confederates. He points toward a horseman (*background*) and makes him famous with the cry, "There stands Jackson like a stone wall!" The Rebels swept the field and "fed fat for days" on the lunches left by fleeing picnickers who had come from Washington to watch the battle.

On to Richmond—and back

General George B. McClellan suffered from agonies of indecision and caution. It took him eight months to organize his invasion of Virginia and to get his massive army ferried into position on the Yorktown Peninsula. Then, though he met only spotty resistance, it took him two months to traverse the 70-odd

miles to Richmond's outskirts. But "Little Mac" showed he knew how to move after the Rebels struck at Mechanicsville and Gaines's Mill on June 26-27, 1862, in the first of the Seven Days' battles. He withdrew so hastily that 2,500 hospitalized troops were left at Savage's Station. His vast supply convoy is seen here struggling safely across Bear Creek, with mounted officers (foreground) exhorting the men onward. Nearing the Union gunboats in the James River, McClellan wired Washington his plaintive epitaph to the inglorious Peninsular Campaign: "I shall do my best to save the army. Send more gunboats."

A BRIDGE AT ANTIETAM is taken by Burnside's troops at a vital moment in the battle on September 17, 1862. In previous assaults the Federals, bunched up at the narrow span, had been mowed down and hurled back. But though Lee repelled the Union attacks, he lost the cream of his army in the process and "sprung the arch upon which the Confederate cause rested."

A BRIDGE AT FREDERICKSBURG is built by Union engineers in the face of fire from across the Rappahannock. By the time Union troops crossed the river, Lee was at full strength on fortified heights. Then Burnside sent his men on their doomed charge. Said a reporter, "It can hardly be in human nature for men to show more valor, or generals to manifest less judgment."

Lee and Burnside in combat at the bridges

TWICE in three months Union General Ambrose Burnside fumbled in major battles at river crossings. He made his first mistake in September 1862. That month McClellan moved across Maryland and cut off an invasion by Lee. The armies met at Antietam Creek, and Corps Commander Burnside was ordered to engage Lee's right flank. Instead of fording the shallow creek, Burnside spent the morning trying to cross a convenient stone bridge (*opposite, top*). Meanwhile the Confederates were able to beat back furious Union attacks on their left and center. When Burnside finally got across the bridge at great cost of life, his men met deadly fire.

Despite this poor performance Burnside was named to replace McClellan, who had let Lee escape at Antietam. In December the armies confronted each other again, at Fredericksburg, Virginia. Burnside, though unnerved by responsibilities he did not want, felt he must attack. But while he waited for pontoons to build bridges over the Rappahannock (*opposite, below*), the Rebels made their position impregnable. Thousands of Northerners died in a brave but fruitless assault on Marye's Heights. "We forgot they were fighting us," Confederate General Pickett wrote his wife, "and cheer after cheer at their fearlessness went up all along our lines."

Dashing troopers of Jeb Stuart's cavalry mark time before Antietam. In the battle they helped rout a Union assault on Lee's left flank.

Bold Rebel attacks of the second day at Gettysburg show early promise in Hood's charge (left) through the Wheat Field and the Peach

A fateful collision
at a Pennsylvania town

In the summer of 1863 Lee again invaded the North. On July 1 a vanguard of his army headed for the town of Gettysburg, Pennsylvania, to capture some new shoes. Around 8 a.m. it bumped into a Union patrol. Help for both sides kept rushing up and clashing all day long. Soon Lee and General George Meade were committed to fighting one of the great battles of U.S. history at

Leaving Gettysburg, a rain-swept Union column files off to the south in a vain, tardy pursuit of Lee's battered army. Up ahead, in a

Orchard. But toward dark, Rebels storming Culp's Hill (center) are repulsed, and so are others battling to stay on Cemetery Hill (right).

this spot. The key decision at Gettysburg was Meade's first—to fight on the defense. In three days Lee vainly dashed wave after valiant wave against the tough Union lines—at Culp's Hill, at Cemetery Ridge, at the Round Tops. When it was over, the Rebels' spendthrift gallantry had garnered 25,000 casualties, nothing more.

On July 4, the fighting did not start up again. The two armies simply stared at each other across the battlefield while a driving rain "washed the blood from the grass." Then Lee and his army began their grim retreat to Virginia. As usual, Union pursuit *(below)* was ineffective. But that day in the West Vicksburg finally fell to Grant. The Confederate cause had just suffered two staggering blows from which it would never recover.

nightmarish race to the Potomac, rolled the endless Confederate convoy—17 miles of cannon and wagons packed with screaming wounded.

A Union tide at Chattanooga

In the fall of 1863 Union General W. S. Rosecrans permitted his army to be trapped in Chattanooga, despite a stubborn stand by General George H. Thomas at the Battle of Chickamauga. Lincoln sent his best general, U. S. Grant, to take over. Grant promptly prepared to attack. On November 24 the Fed-

erals seized Lookout Mountain, one of several heights from which Confederate artillery dominated the city. As low clouds lifted, watchers saw blue-clad troops advancing on topmost Pulpit Rock (above). But the key hill was Missionary Ridge, and next day Grant sent Thomas' superb troops to take the rifle pits below it. They took the pits—and kept on up the slope, yelling "Chickamauga!" "Who ordered those men up the ridge?" Grant demanded angrily. An officer said simply, "When those fellows get started all hell can't stop them." By day's end the Rebels had been routed; the road to Atlanta lay open (next page).

"THE VANDAL CHIEF," a name Sherman was called by the outraged Southerners, leads his staff (right) in a grand review at Savannah. Actually, the Southern epithet applied with more accuracy to General Judson Kilpatrick (fourth from left), who with his greedy cavalrymen made off with a fortune in plunder.

Sherman's raiders go marching through Georgia

ON Grant's elevation to commander in chief, his trusted and brilliant lieutenant in the West, William T. Sherman, was assigned a 100,000-man army and a chance to prove one of his favorite contentions: "Pierce the shell of the C.S.A., and it's all hollow inside." Plunging into Georgia in May 1864, Sherman followed Grant's orders "to move against Johnston's army." Though he did not manage "to break it up," he did much better at "inflicting all the damage you can." On September 2 he took Atlanta. Then on November 15 he cast loose from his base and headed for the coast in the famous march to the sea, living off the land and cutting a broad swath of ruin (*left*) all the way to the coast. Triumphantly he presented the city of Savannah to Lincoln for Christmas. Finally, estimating his damages to date at $100 million, he turned north to wreak even greater havoc on South Carolina.

YANKEE WRECKERS tear up Rebel rails—merely metal strips on a wood base—during Sherman's march from Atlanta to the sea. Nothing that might be used for "warlike purposes" was spared, but Sherman saw his chief mission as breaking the will of civilians to continue the fight.

RACING TO SPOTSYLVANIA, a Union battery (above) struggles through gluey mud to join the sprawling 14-day campaign. Its crucial action developed at "Bloody Angle," a weak point in the Confederate line where Grant tried to split Lee's army in half. He narrowly failed, and 12,000 Rebels and Federals fell in one day of point-blank volleying and hand-to-hand combat.

FLEEING IN THE WILDERNESS, litter bearers save a fallen comrade from a forest fire set by gun blasts in the dry brush. Many of the wounded on both sides burned to death in the holocaust.

A murderous Maytime in the dark forests of Virginia

GENERAL U.S. GRANT was a hard-bitten realist. When he launched his Virginia offensive in May 1864, he expected to pay a high price to bring Lee to book. The price was, in fact, staggering. The Wilderness, a "bloody hunt to the death," cost him 17,500 casualties, Spotsylvania another 18,400. At Cold Harbor, lacking room to flank Lee, he ordered a frontal attack (*below*) and sacrificed 7,000 men in half an hour. These losses appalled the North. But Grant was keeping Lee heavily engaged, bleeding him white while preventing escape or counteroffensive. In this brutal bludgeoning, said one of Lee's staff, Grant had found "the only way that the strength of such an army, so commanded, could be destroyed."

ATTACKING AT COLD HARBOR, Union skirmishers (*below*) draw a storm of shot from impregnable trenchworks. At battle's end, the corpses covered five acres.

Great leaders of a lost cause

The terrible attrition that wore away Lee's troops cut down his top officers as well. Through much of the war, the Confederacy had many brilliant generals. They are shown above at their zenith. Among them were Hood (*extreme left*), Ewell (foot on stump), Jackson (in profile, mounted), Hill (leaning on

sword), Lee himself *(center)*, Longstreet (holding fieldglasses), Stuart *(far right)*. But as Lee neared Appomattox in April 1865, only a few of his old commanders were left for him to lean on. Hood had been maimed and Ewell captured. Jackson and Hill were dead. Longstreet was still with Lee, but Stuart had died.

With his command shattered, with his once-mighty army reduced to 25,000 shambling survivors, Lee surrendered on April 9. As he needlessly explained to his men, there was no shame in yielding "to overwhelming numbers and resources." Obviously, they had worked a military miracle in resisting so long.

5. THE AVENGING NORTH

THE handsome young man with the strained face leaped from the theater box onto the stage, paused to glare at the audience and then disappeared into the wings. The crowd at Ford's Theater in Washington sat silent and puzzled. Suddenly a woman's scream rang out, and then from all over the theater people began to shout the awful truth: "He has shot the President."

It was April 14, 1865, and John Wilkes Booth had just consummated one of the great tragedies in American history—the assassination of Abraham Lincoln. Confused motives had thronged Booth's cloudy mind, but one stood out with something resembling clarity. He thought that by removing Lincoln he was in some way helping his defeated South.

He had not, of course, helped the South at all; he had in fact hurt it. The striking down of the great war leader at the moment of victory aroused a display of mass emotion scarcely equaled before or since in the United States. A special funeral train bore Lincoln's body home to Springfield across a mourning country, "through day and night," in Walt Whitman's words, "with the great cloud darkening the land."

The death and the funeral march evoked both deep grief and savage anger. Immediately men assumed that Jefferson Davis and other Southern leaders had instigated the crime. "It was Slavery that conceived the fearful deed; it was Slavery that sought and found the willing instrument and sped the fatal ball," one newspaper accused. Secretary of War Stanton, supplying the press

A TORMENTED PRESIDENT, Andrew Johnson, an advocate of a moderate Reconstruction program, is remembered now as the 19th Century President who was impeached.

with official dispatches, fanned the wild suspicions. Evidence had been found, he announced, that the crime was the result of a conspiracy "planned and set on foot by rebels." The cry went up that the South must be punished.

By his act Booth had damaged the hopes of the entire nation for an easy "reconstruction." This was a term applied by men of the postwar period to the situation they confronted in 1865 and after. The 11 states of the Confederacy had been defeated in war; now they had to be brought back into the Union. But this raised many questions. Should they be forced to conform to certain conditions? How would a democratic government enforce a program of reform upon a conquered people? Could it, in fact, impose such a program if the Southern states still had all the rights of states? And what of the almost four million slaves freed as a result of the war? Should they have civil rights and suffrage immediately or should they be held for a time in some status between complete freedom and servitude? And specifically, who should determine their status, the central government or the Southern states?

On April 20, 1865, this poster was issued offering $100,000 for the capture of John Wilkes Booth and his cohorts. Six days later federal agents trapped Booth; he was dying, whether from their bullets or his own no one knows. Following a great dispute, the reward was finally split 53 ways.

BOOTH had shot the one man who might have provided the leadership needed so urgently at this unique moment in U.S. history. Lincoln had thought much about the problem. In December 1863 he had advanced what is familiarly called his plan of Reconstruction. Under his authority to issue pardons, he had proffered a general amnesty to all who would take an oath of loyalty to the United States and recognize the wartime acts and proclamations concerning slavery. Men who had held high office in the Confederacy could not take the oath; these individuals Lincoln apparently meant to exclude until the passions of war had cooled and they could be safely pardoned. Whenever in any state 10 per cent or more of the voters of 1860 swore the oath, they could set up a government and send representatives to Congress.

Several features of Lincoln's scheme deserve analysis. He was willing to start the restoration process in any state even if only a minority took the oath. In proposing to return Southern—and presumably Democratic—delegations immediately to Congress, he was not thinking very much about the effects of restoration on Republican fortunes. Most remarkably, Lincoln did not propose to establish any official control of race relations by the national government—and did not require formal state abolition of slavery to finish the job started by the Emancipation Proclamation. Instead, in communications to civil leaders and to his military commanders in the occupied Confederate states of Tennessee, Arkansas and Louisiana, he urged that slavery should be abolished and suggested extending suffrage to some blacks, those who were of the greatest intelligence or had served in the Union armies.

All three states acted to return under Lincoln's plan in 1864. But Congress refused to admit their delegates or to record their electoral votes in that year's presidential election. In effect, the legislative branch—and the Republican majority—repudiated the President's plan.

This rejection resulted from diverse and not always consistent motives. Some legislators considered Reconstruction strictly the business of Congress. Others wondered about the constitutional status of the seceded states. Many felt that Lincoln's plan did not provide adequate protection for the freed slaves. There was also a general feeling that Reconstruction was being made too easy, that unrepentant Southerners might soon be strutting in the halls of Washington. Most angered were the Radical Republicans, whose leaders were convinced that the softhearted President was not, in the words of one editor, "the man to handle this country, while its heart is over-generous with reconstituted peace, so that due guarantees may be exacted from its enemies."

Two Radical leaders, "Bluff Ben" Wade of the Senate and Henry Winter Davis of the House, hastily proposed a more stringent alternative to Lincoln's plan and drove it through Congress in July 1864. The Wade-Davis measure assumed that the seceded states were out of the Union. For each conquered state the President was to appoint a provisional governor. If a *majority* of the state's white males took a loyalty oath, the governor could call an election for a constitutional convention. But not all who had sworn the oath could vote for delegates—only those who could further swear the "ironclad oath" that they had never voluntarily borne arms against the United States or aided the Confederacy. Each constitution must contain provisions abolishing slavery, disfranchising Confederate leaders and repudiating Confederate and state war debts. After these conditions were met, the state would be readmitted.

Lincoln objected to the Wade-Davis measure on several grounds and most strongly to the provision requiring states to abolish slavery. Slavery could be abolished, Lincoln contended, only by action of individual states or by amending the Constitution. He disposed of the bill with a pocket veto and gave his reasons in a sharply worded statement. Wade and Davis responded with a blistering "Manifesto" charging that "a more studied outrage on the legislative authority of the people" had "never been perpetrated."

The episode caused Lincoln to take new stock of the situation. He sensed now that Northern opinion would not agree to his simple plan. He was still considering some new approach to the problem—though its nature was never revealed—when Booth fired his fatal shot.

ALL the politicians who proposed plans of Reconstruction had to consider Northern opinion. Many Northerners came out of the ordeal of the war with feelings of hostility, even of hatred, for Southerners. At the least they demanded of the South some evidence of regret for the past and loyalty for the future. "We hold," said one editor, "that repentance . . . should go before absolution and perfect pardon." Most Northerners felt the government had an obligation to assure the blacks real freedom; others saw an opportunity to reform the South along Northern lines.

A majority of Northerners were Republicans, and in the last analysis the pattern of Reconstruction would be determined by Republican politicians. These men approached the problem with varying motives. An immediate return of the 11 Confederate states would produce an influx of Democrats into Congress that would cut into the Republican majorities and might threaten the economic legislation of the war years—such as the protective tariff and the National Bank system—prized by Northern pressure groups.

Most congressional Republicans favored some kind of limited suffrage for the blacks, to be extended by national action. "I admit the negroes are not intelligent enough to vote," said Senator John Sherman of Ohio, "[but] how much more ignorant are these slaves than the uneducated white people down South?" But Congress was restrained on this issue for the moment by doubt that Northern opinion would accept Negro suffrage even for the South. Only six states—Wisconsin, Vermont, Maine, New Hampshire, Massachusetts and Rhode Island—permitted blacks to vote without restriction. In 1867 Ohio,

Eliza McCardle (above) was 17 when young Andrew Johnson, unknown and semiliterate, rode into Greeneville, Tennessee, in 1826. She watched his entrance with a group of her friends and admitted that she already liked the boy. Within a year the two were married; she later taught him to write and figure.

As a tailor in Greeneville, the youthful Andrew Johnson worked and lived in this cramped two-room building on Main Street. Four people dwelled here in a space described as "ten feet square": Johnson, his wife Eliza and their children, Charles and Martha. They moved out after four years.

Michigan, Minnesota, Kansas and Connecticut rejected proposals for Negro suffrage.

The most ardent advocates of a drastic Reconstruction process were the Radicals. In the House their leader was Thaddeus Stevens of Pennsylvania—"Old Thad," bewigged, clubfooted and sardonically bitter. In the Senate their chiefs were Wade, the idealistic Charles Sumner and Zachariah Chandler of Michigan, passionate, vituperative and grimly devoted to the interest of his party and Northern business. The Radicals urged that the late leaders of the Confederacy be excluded from political life, that numbers of Southern whites be disfranchised, that the property of rich Rebels be confiscated and distributed among the freedmen and that suffrage be placed in "loyal" black hands. "This must be done," cried Stevens, "even though it drive [the South's] nobility into exile. If they go, all the better."

Although the Radicals argued that the rebellious states had lost their constitutional identity, most Republicans were as yet not willing to go that length. Instead the party leaders talked about the doctrine of "forfeited rights." By seceding, the states had lost some of their rights. They should be kept out of the Union until they had demonstrated a proper spirit of repentance. How much repentance they would have to display would depend on a number of factors, most notably on the spirit demonstrated by Southerners and on the leadership of the man who succeeded Lincoln as President—the Vice President, who in the turmoil following Lincoln's death was sworn in as chief executive.

No inheritor of the presidential title assumed office under stranger conditions than Andrew Johnson. A Southerner, a former slaveholder and a Democrat, he had been placed on the ticket with Lincoln in 1864 to attract the votes of other Democrats. In the past he had served his state of Tennessee as governor, in the House and in the Senate. On all possible occasions he had voiced the aspirations of the small white farmers of the South and had denounced in unmeasured terms the planter aristocracy. "Some day," he once threatened, "I will show the stuck-up aristocrats who is running the country."

When Tennessee left the Union, Johnson remained in the Senate and stigmatized secession as treason. After Federal forces occupied most of Tennessee, he accepted an appointment from Lincoln as military governor of the state and held the office for three years amid great physical peril. He was the most prominent Southern advocate of the Union, and to the Northern public something of a hero. His black eyes bored out from a rugged face; everything about him seemed to embody honesty and rough, uncompromising courage.

But despite his reputation, in almost every way Johnson was unfit to be President during the dark and dangerous crisis of Reconstruction. He was a dogmatic states' righter who had always fought measures to increase federal power. For example, he had voted in Congress against the establishment of the Smithsonian Institution, arguing that government funds should not be used to foster even so desirable an activity as science. Such a man could have no sympathy for the basic Republican concepts: that the government had an obligation to do something for ex-slaves and to stimulate the economy with beneficent legislation. Johnson was quite ready to concede that some blacks should have the vote, but he insisted that under the Constitution the privilege could be bestowed on them only by the states. His devotion to the Constitution was sincere, but it was also a real weakness. He construed the

This New England "schoolma'am" is one of thousands who flocked south after the war to teach freed slaves. Southern whites bitterly resented the intruders, even resorting to violence to drive them out. One teacher whose school was repeatedly stoned found an effective countermeasure: older pupils were told to come to class carrying arms. The stoning promptly stopped.

fundamental law in a narrow, legalistic fashion, forgetting that a document of 1787 could not apply to every future situation.

Johnson was, in essence, a man of abstractions and morality rather than a man of politics. He could not compromise and hence he could not lead. Suspicious and secretive, he saw plots to destroy him on every hand. Richard Taylor, a former Rebel general who had good reason to support Johnson's policies, commented of his personality: "Like a badger, one had to dig him out of his hole; and he was ever in one except when on the hustings addressing the crowd."

Certain of himself and of his principles, Johnson proclaimed his own plan of Reconstruction. He accepted the restoration of the Lincoln states—the three his predecessor had been willing to welcome back—and also of Virginia, where he recognized a Unionist governor. In the seven remaining Confederate states amnesty was offered to all who would take a loyalty oath. Excluded from the privilege pending presidential pardon were high civil and military leaders of the Confederacy—and former rebels worth $20,000 or more, a measure presumably aimed at Johnson's old planter enemies. After the registration of voters, Johnson expected the next step to be the convoking of a state convention, which had to nullify the ordinance of secession, abolish slavery and repudiate the Confederate and state war debts. Johnson's plan, although in some respects like Lincoln's, was more similar to the Wade-Davis bill. But it soon was apparent that the Republicans had moved beyond Wade-Davis.

Johnson had executed his plan during the summer of 1865 when Congress was not in session. When the legislators convened in December, they found representatives from eight Southern states demanding admission to Congress. The identities of some of these men shocked the North. Among them were four generals, five colonels, six cabinet officials, 58 congressmen of the old Confederacy—and, as a Georgia senator, Alexander H. Stephens, late Confederate Vice President. Eight months before, many of these men had been in arms against the Union; now, it seemed to Republicans, they were ready to construe the Constitution to its defenders. The Republican majority angrily denied admission to all these delegations. Then Congress appointed a joint committee of both houses to advise on the framing of a restoration program.

W HILE this Committee on Reconstruction took testimony early in 1866, events in the Southern states further aroused Northern opinion. At a number of places collisions occurred between the races. In a riot at New Orleans, 48 Republicans—mostly blacks—were killed and 166 wounded by city police. In Memphis a fight between black soldiers and city police developed into a pitched battle in which 46 blacks were killed and a number of buildings burned. Johnson expressed no public shock at the violence, and Northerners wondered if his easy restoration policy had not encouraged Southern whites to think they could intimidate the freedmen into a position of servitude.

Confirming this impression were the laws passed by the Johnson and Lincoln states known as the Black Codes. These acts were designed to control both the economic and the social status of the Negroes. All of them extended certain rights to the freedmen—to hold property, make contracts, to sue and be sued. All of them denied blacks certain rights—to serve on juries, bear arms, engage in mass meetings. Blacks could not testify against whites or could do so only under restricted conditions. Separate public school systems were prescribed. All of the codes contained provisions designed to force the

Radical Benjamin Wade, who once called Lincoln "a man sprung from poor white trash," at first thought Andrew Johnson an improvement. "There will be no trouble in running the government now," he exulted. But Wade was soon a leader in the fight to oust Johnson. If he had succeeded, Wade would have jumped from president pro tem of the Senate to President of the U.S.

freedmen into labor arrangements. Negroes without employment could be arrested as vagrants and hired out to employers. In some states blacks could engage only in "husbandry," which included field labor and house service.

Whatever the economic clauses of the Black Codes seemed to the South, they seemed to the North to inaugurate a system of peonage. "We tell the men of Mississippi," declared a Chicago newspaper, "that the men of the North will convert . . . Mississippi into a frog pond before they will allow such laws."

Concern for the fate of the former slaves was heightened when Johnson vetoed a bill extending the life of the Freedmen's Bureau, an agency created near the end of the war to help the blacks make the transition to freedom. In his usual narrow fashion, Johnson pointed out that the Constitution did not sanction creation of a federal agency to exercise functions of relief. Even moderate Republicans were upset—but for the moment the veto was narrowly sustained. However, not long afterward another Freedmen's Bureau bill was passed over Johnson's veto. Between those two bills a great deal happened.

ON the night of February 22, 1866, a crowd came to the White House to hear the President speak. At first he tried to speak moderately, but the lure of the cheering crowd was too much for him. Suddenly he dropped the role of President Johnson and became again Andy Johnson, the Tennessee stump speaker. There were disunionists in the North, he cried, fully as dangerous as the former seceders; he named among others Stevens and Sumner. Then he launched into a tirade in which he hinted that the Radicals wanted him assassinated. It was a painful performance, revealing a man who was fast losing touch with reality. The Radicals were infuriated, the moderates shocked.

Reaction was not long in coming. In March Congress enacted the Civil Rights bill. Designed to invalidate the Black Codes, it forbade states to discriminate against citizens on account of race. Johnson vetoed it on the ground that it violated the rights of the states. Congress overrode the veto by one vote. Clearly the moderates were leaving Johnson.

At this critical point the Committee on Reconstruction brought forward its long, studied plan of restoration. Cast in the form of a proposed amendment to the Constitution, the 14th, it was neither completely a Radical nor a Conservative product. It was a compromise, and it represented, perhaps, the last chance for agreement between the President and the Congress.

The 14th Amendment had four important sections. One provided the first national definition of citizenship—all persons born or naturalized in the United States were citizens of the nation and of the state where they resided. No state could abridge the rights of a citizen or deprive any person of life, liberty or property without due process of law.

The second section dealt with the curious effect of emancipation on Southern representation in the House of Representatives and the electoral college. The Constitution had provided that in determining the population of a state for purposes of representation all the free inhabitants were to be counted, plus three fifths of the slaves. But now there were no slaves; all blacks would be counted in full, and the Confederate states would pick up at least 12 additional representatives. To the Republicans this seemed a perversion of justice and of the results of the war. Therefore it was decided that if any state denied the suffrage to any part of its adult male population the representation of that state should be reduced in proportion. (The reduction clause

Though Secretary of War Stanton advocated harsh Reconstruction, in his youth he had been quite a gay blade. As a student at Kenyon, he once wrote a friend that while "in chase of a petticoat" he had become so bedazzled he lost his way home and stayed out all night, becoming ill of exposure. "So much for love," Stanton concluded. "Rather expensive, don't you think so?"

was not effectively applied for almost a century; then it was made the basis for a suit by black leaders in 1963.)

The third section disqualified from national or state office, but not from voting, all persons who in any official capacity had taken an oath to uphold the Constitution and then had engaged in or supported rebellion. These men were to be disbarred until pardoned by a two-thirds vote of both houses of Congress.

The fourth section validated the United States debt and invalidated the Confederate debt.

The 14th Amendment was submitted for ratification to all the states—including those lately in rebellion and which the Radicals held were not fully in the Union. Back of this apparent paradox was a fear that the ratification process would not be legal unless submitted to the total number of states. President Johnson let it be known that he hoped the measure would be defeated. The Southern states needed no presidential urging. The South would not vote to place a stigma on its recent leaders. "If we are to be degraded," wrote a conservative North Carolinian, "we will retain some self-esteem by not making it abasement." As there were 37 states, the votes of 10 could defeat the amendment. Of the Confederate states, only Tennessee, controlled by personal enemies of Johnson, ratified (and won readmittance as a reward). The other 10 plus Kentucky and Delaware voted against the amendment, and they were enough to defeat it.

The amendment was lost but only for the moment. Later it would be brought up again and ratified. Now its defeat strengthened the Radicals and their demands for a harsher policy. "They would not cooperate with us in rebuilding what they destroyed," exclaimed an indignant Republican congressman. "We must remove the rubbish and rebuild from the bottom."

On his ill-starred "swing 'round the circle" in 1866, President Johnson speaks from the rear of his special train. On the trip he traded insults with hecklers, but none matched the invective hurled at him by the opposition press. One religious journal called his eyes "lascivious" and said Johnson was "touched with insanity, corrupted with lust, stimulated with drink."

THE hardening of Northern opinion was apparent in the congressional campaign of 1866. It was a bitter and crucial contest. Radical speakers denounced Johnson as "worse than Judas Iscariot or Benedict Arnold," as an "insolent drunken brute" and as a "calamitous and traitorous Executive."

Johnson fought back. Embarking on an 18-day speaking tour, he resorted to his old stump-speaking invective and shouted once again that Stevens, Sumner and other Radicals were traitors. The Radicals planted hecklers at some of his meetings, and these men trapped him into undignified shouting matches. At Indianapolis his audience degenerated into a rioting mob. Shots were fired, and one man was killed. Johnson had hurt his cause instead of helping it. The elections returned huge Republican majorities. Congress could now move to impose on the South any Reconstruction plan it desired.

The assured Radicals moved with remorseless zeal. They pushed through Congress three acts, all of them vetoed by Johnson and easily repassed. These Reconstruction Acts of 1867 constituted the Radicals' final plan of Reconstruction. Boldly the new laws obliterated state identities. The Lincoln-Johnson governments were declared to have no legal status, and the 10 former Confederate states—Tennessee was now out of it—were combined into five military districts. In command of each district or "conquered province" was an army general. Congress could not legally prescribe suffrage requirements for a state, but presumably it could for military districts. Hence registrars were directed to register all adult males without reference to color. (Not surprisingly, the registration enrolled more blacks than whites.) After the registration the voters of a province were to elect a convention to prepare a state constitution—which had to include a provision establishing Negro suffrage, and thus legalizing the doubtful action of Congress. If the voters ratified the constitution, elections could be held to set up a state government. Then, if the legislature endorsed the 14th Amendment and if Congress approved the constitution, the state might be readmitted. By the end of 1868, six of the Confederate states had completed the process and were back in the Union. By mid-1870 all had been restored.

As the Radicals drove through their program, people all over the North asked an inevitable question: If it was right that blacks in the South have the suffrage, why not blacks everywhere? Accordingly Congress framed another amendment, the 15th, which forbade states to deny suffrage because of color. It went into effect in 1870, marking a result few had foreseen. In the beginning most Republicans had favored only a grant of limited Negro suffrage. But they had presumed to deal with a great abstract issue that could not be limited. Finally the issue had taken over from the politicians and forced its own way to its own conclusion.

In 1867 the Radicals were at the height of their power, and in their triumphant hour they reached out for still more victories. Because they controlled Congress, they considered that branch the central power of the government. Congress, said Thaddeus Stevens, was sovereign: "No Government official, from the President and Chief Justice down, can do any one act which is not prescribed and directed by the legislative power."

The Supreme Court drew the suspicious attention of the Radicals. In 1866, in the case of *ex parte Milligan*, it declared the military courts of the war years had been unconstitutional in areas where civic courts were in operation. When the Court followed up by agreeing to hear a case involving the validity of military courts in Mississippi, the Radical majority passed a law withdrawing the justices' appellate jurisdiction in cases concerning habeas corpus. Without protest the Court abandoned its review. "The court stood still to be ravished and did not even hallo while the thing was being done," said one observer contemptuously.

But the greatest institutional obstacle to the Radicals was the presidency. To subordinate the executive branch, and specifically Johnson, the Radicals forced through two laws, both clearly in violation of the Constitution. The Tenure of Office Act forbade the President to remove civil officials, including members of his Cabinet, without the consent of the Senate. It was intended, among other things, to protect Secretary of War Stanton, who was important to the Radicals as the supervisor of the army's work in the South. Stanton openly disagreed with Johnson and surreptitiously aided the Radicals, yet he would not resign; he was convinced that he had to stay on to protect the fruits of the war from Rebel ravage.

The Command of the Army Act prohibited the President from issuing orders to the army except through the commanding general. This was Grant, who supported the concept of military control of the South. The Radicals were deliberately creating an imbalance of power in the American system.

After 1867 Johnson, effectively hamstrung, was more of an irritation than a menace to the Radicals. Nevertheless, their detestation of him had grown so great that they would go to any length to humiliate him. The supreme

Defying colleagues and constituents, Senator Edmund Ross voted "not guilty" at Andrew Johnson's impeachment. He lost the next election, and it took 20 years for those who branded him "traitor and poltroon" to admit that by guarding the presidency, he had helped prevent a "calamity greater than war."

Aged and frail, Representative Thaddeus Stevens is carried to the trial of Andrew Johnson. During the proceedings he declared that if the President were not removed, the Republican party would die and the country would be given over to the "so-called Democracy, which is worse than the devil."

abasement would be to remove him from office. The only way to achieve this was by impeachment, and the Constitution stated that the only impeachable offenses were the commission of high crimes and misdemeanors. Hopefully the Radicals sought for evidence. They considered all manner of wild rumors —that Johnson had been guilty of treason during the war, or had had some part in the assassination of Lincoln, or as President had sold pardons. They could find nothing that would stick.

Suddenly Johnson himself gave them a pretext. He suspended Secretary Stanton from office. When the Senate, acting under the Tenure of Office Act, refused to concur, the President removed Stanton outright. The Radicals moved quickly to exploit the situation.

The House framed and presented to the Senate, the constitutional body to hear impeachment proceedings, 11 charges against Johnson. Nine dealt with the violation of the Tenure of Office Act. The last two accused the President of defaming Congress in his speeches and bringing it into popular disrespect, and of not faithfully executing the Reconstruction law. Johnson would be removed from his high office if two thirds of the senators, or 36, voted that he was guilty. The Republican majority counted 42 senators, the opposition consisted of 12 Democrats.

T HE trial began in March 1868. It was conducted with impressive ceremony. Chief Justice Salmon P. Chase presided. Five able lawyers represented Johnson. Seven managers were named by the House to present the charges. The most colorful of the House managers was Benjamin F. Butler. Rotund, bald, with drooping lids, and looking, it was said, like "a cross-eyed cuttlefish," Butler did most of the speaking for the prosecution. But the dominating spirit among the managers was Thad Stevens. So feeble that at least once he had to be carried into the Senate chamber in a chair, the old man had only a few months to live. But this was to be his hour.

At first the drama of the trial attracted undivided public attention. But it wore on too long—through April and then into May. People wearied of the lengthy speeches and the complicated questioning of witnesses. Butler damaged the prosecution case with an absurd charge that Johnson had tried to set up a dictatorship. The President's lawyers helped his cause by sticking to a purely legal defense. Only when the vote was taken did the drama return. The House managers, by now sensing the weakness of their case, asked first for a test on the 11th charge, a catchall that included all the major accusations against Johnson. In a tense atmosphere the roll was called. It disclosed 35 votes for "guilty" and 19 for "not guilty." The Radicals had fallen one vote short. Frantically the House managers asked for an adjournment of 10 days. In the interim every type of pressure was brought to bear on the seven Republican senators who had dared oppose the lash of party discipline. They would not budge. At the next session two more of the charges were brought to a vote. The result was the same. Chase adjourned the proceedings, and the Radicals, recognizing defeat, sullenly acquiesced.

The Radicals might feel frustration at their failure to humble Johnson, but they had no cause to fear him. He was no more than a prisoner in his office and in less than a year would depart the scene. The fabric of Radical Reconstruction was enshrined in laws that seemed beyond repeal. And the reality of Republican rule was to all appearances firmly fastened on the South.

When it began, President Johnson's trial was the best show in the nation. Reporters covered it like a murder case (below), and tickets (above) were in such demand that one Washington woman awakened a congressman at midnight and refused to leave his house until he had promised to get her admitted.

CARPETBAG RULE is lampooned in an 1880 cartoon of U.S. Grant riding on the back of the burdened South. The derisive term "carpetbagger"—ostensibly a stranger who arrives in town carrying all he owns in one satchel —dated back to the 1840s.

THE AFTERMATH OF WAR is seen in this Charleston neighborhood. The city was swept by fire in 1861 and hammered by Union artillery from 1863 on. This picture, taken in April 1865, shows scaffolding up and the city already in the throes of Reconstruction.

The bitter postscript to defeat

THE true extent of the South's defeat was to be measured not in the cold statistics of property damaged or numbers of dead, but in the hearts of the survivors. "Our fields everywhere lie untilled," wrote a Mississippian. "Childless old age, widows, and helpless orphans beggared and hopeless, are everywhere." Even for those not in want, the situation seemed appalling. Southerners felt humiliated and hopeless. Federal troops patrolled Southern streets. Northern civilians poured into the region and took a vigorous part in Reconstruction activities. A number of high positions in state governments were occupied by men who had until a short time before been slaves.

The white men of the South reacted in two ways. Some tried sturdily to make the best of things. "The war being at an end," said R. E. Lee, "I believe it to be the duty of everyone to unite in the restoration of the country." But others nursed their hatred: George E. Pickett coldly turned down a position as a U.S. marshal offered him by President Grant, and Nathan Bedford Forrest became a leader of the harshly anti-Negro Ku-Klux Klan. Slowly a new South began to emerge, quite different from the one that had once existed.

A TOBACCO FIELD yields new wealth for the emerging South. Cultivation of this crop was widespread throughout the upper South after the war, and it furnished a vital source of revenue.

A LUMBERYARD in Louisiana reflects the swift growth of the timber industry during Reconstruction. By 1900 turpentine alone was to bring more than $20 million to the Deep South.

New crops and old build a foundation for recovery

FOR half a century the South's economy had been firmly founded on cotton. When cotton boomed, the South boomed. Now as the region struggled to regain its feet, cotton was still the crop it depended on most. But the fiber was unstable in production and price, and insects and weather could play havoc with entire fields. Seeking to free itself from its one-crop economy, the postwar South diversified. Cotton gins were rebuilt, but new crops and industries were encouraged as well. Tobacco raising flourished. Sawmills and turpentine distilleries were constructed. Southern businessmen set up partnerships with Northerners in merchandising and manufacturing. But agriculture was handicapped by the ending of slavery—by 1869 cheap labor was so scarce that some Southern planters imported Chinese coolies to work the fields. Nonetheless, a few thoughtful men welcomed the end of the "peculiar institution." "It is the white man of the South more than the black," said one historian, "that has been freed by the Civil War."

A COTTON BOAT steams to market bearing a heavy cargo, a common postwar scene on Southern rivers. In the months just after Appomattox, cotton prices went as high as $125 a bale.

KLAN REGALIA is displayed by a member of the secret order. In these uniforms, called "shrouds," Klansmen pretended to be the spirits of dead Rebel soldiers just come from hell.

SOUTHERN AVENGERS of the Big Poplar, North Carolina, Ku-Klux Klan prepare to hang John Campbell for being an ardent

Predominantly black, the House of Representatives in South

Background for strife: Negroes in office

WITH many Southern whites disfranchised, blacks soon sat in every Southern legislature (although they held a majority of seats only in one state). But they had no fund of experience or education—under the old slave codes it was illegal for Negroes even to be taught to read or write. The black lawmakers often struggled in vain simply to cope with parliamentary procedure. Many white Southerners fiercely resented seeing ex-slaves in positions of power. The Ku Klux Klan was one response. By threats and violence, Klansmen frightened blacks from the polls. By 1877 Southern whites had returned to power throughout the old Confederacy.

Republican. Before the execution could take place, federal agents appeared, dispersed the Klansmen and rescued Campbell.

Carolina meets in 1876, near Reconstruction's end.

BLACK POLITICIANS dominate a photo of Louisiana legislators. Pinckney Pinchback *(bottom, center)* later was acting governor, the highest state post held by a Negro in the postwar South.

A RACE RIOT pits whites against blacks in Charleston, South Carolina, on June 24, 1866. The sketch, made on the scene by a *Harper's* artist, shows an officer's futile effort to halt the melee.

Out of the violence the promise of a new start

SIX years separate the scenes above and at right. They had been turbulent years, made so by the reaction of Southerners to what an Alabama editor called "the galling despotism that broods like a nightmare over these Southern States." In 1865 returning Rebels found themselves clerking in stores that served former slaves or cleaning and re-laying bricks from charred rubble. Many resented their new jobs as degrading, but others were taking to heart the words of Charles Henry Smith's fictious character Bill Arp, whose humor had brightened the war's darkness: "Well, I killed as many of them as they did of me, and now I'm going to work." By the 1870s resurgent whites were recovering their power, and Negroes lost the support they needed to stay in office. As Democrats regained one legislature after another and clamped down on the blacks' freedom, the South began to assume the aspect it would wear for another century.

THE BUSTLE OF RECOVERY pervades Charleston in this 1872 painting. The city was regaining its prewar look—except for the presence of the Northern officer at right.

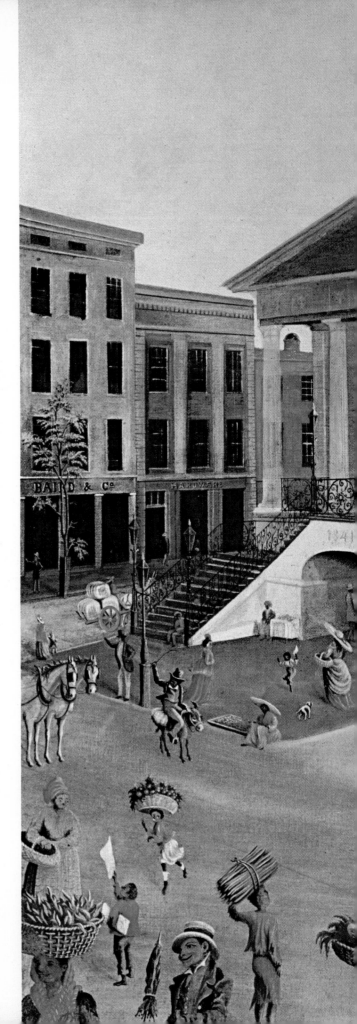

6. THE RAVAGED SOUTH

"THE most terrible part of the war is now to come," wrote a Georgia girl in her diary shortly after Appomattox. "The props that held society up are broken. Everything is in a state of disorganization and tumult. We have no currency, no law save the primitive code that might makes right. We are in a transition state from war to subjugation, and it is far worse than was the transition from peace to war. The suspense and anxiety in which we live are terrible."

Although Union soldiers went home in 1865 at federal expense and were given mustering-out pay, Confederate soldiers had to make their way home as best they could, often having to beg their way "with nothing to exchange for bread save the unwelcome news of Appomattox." They returned to a ravaged region. Sidney Andrews, a New England journalist, traveled to the South later that year and reported his impressions. He saw Charleston: "A city of ruins, of desolation, of vacant houses, of widowed women, of rotting wharves, of deserted warehouses, of weed-wild gardens, of miles of grass-grown streets, of acres of pitiful and voiceful barrenness." He saw Columbia: "It is now a wilderness of ruins. Its heart is but a mass of blackened chimneys and crumbling walls."

The same scenes, with variations, could be seen in the rural areas. A Northern traveler marveled at the marks of Sherman's march through South Carolina: "Many miles like a broad black streak of ruin and desolation—the fences

BACK UNDER THE OLD FLAG, a riverboat in a postwar print loads sugar along the Mississippi as the defeated South takes its first slow steps toward economic recovery.

all gone; lonesome smoke stacks, surrounded by dark heaps of ashes and cinders, marking the spots where human habitations had stood."

For many Southern people by 1865, the problem was, as one Northern observer reported, not how to live comfortably but how to live at all. "Everything has been mended, and generally in the rudest style. Window-glass has given way to thin boards. . . . A complete set of crockery is never seen. . . . Clocks and watches have nearly all stopped."

The devastation of war was not equally intense throughout the South—some states suffered more than others—but it was universal. Economic life in the whole section fell to an almost primitive level. The $85 million or so of Southern banking capital that had existed in 1860 had now vanished. The credit system on which the area's trade and farming depended had been wrecked. Plantation and farm lands lay abandoned or uncultivated. Cities and towns stood in waste or gray depression. Factories were idled or destroyed. Roads and bridges had either been wrecked or were in utter disrepair. The railroad system had collapsed under the strain of war and the blows of Federal raiders. Depots and repair shops had disappeared, crossties were rotted, rails had been bent and burned. The largest rail line in Louisiana had less than 10 per cent of its prewar rolling stock—only four out of 45 locomotives, four of its original 37 passenger cars, 36 of 500 freight cars. Even school and church buildings had felt the hand of war. Lying in the path of the armies, they had been put to damaging use, often as hospitals, or had been destroyed outright.

The direct physical damages of the war were appallingly evident. Not so apparent but still painful were the losses in personal property. Southerners who had invested in Confederate and state bonds saw their savings disappear as the national government forced repudiation of all Rebel war debts. The process of emancipation deprived slaveholders of human property valued at two billion dollars. A special cotton tax imposed by the federal government drained an additional $68 million out of the South.

Southern whites were numbed as they surveyed the wreckage of their civilization. "We are shattered [and] stunned," wrote a South Carolina woman in her diary, "the remnant of heart left alive in us filled with brotherly hate." Of hatred of the victorious Yankees, there was plenty. "They've left me one inestimable privilege—to hate 'em," said an impoverished hotelkeeper. "I git up at half-past four in the morning and sit up till twelve at night to hate 'em."

In a cartoon by Thomas Nast, a Confederate veteran glares sullenly in defeat. A Northern newsman who was visiting the South reported that food was a problem but people were far from contrite. "For breakfast," he said, there was "salt fish, fried potatoes and treason. Fried potatoes, treason and salt fish for dinner," and for supper, "treason, salt fish, fried potatoes."

B UT for thousands of white and black Southerners alike, the immediate concern at the end of the war was not the luxury of hatred but the necessity for survival. Because the hostilities had continued into the spring and the beginning of the planting season, there was a dangerous shortage of food. Poor people of both races had to be fed. The Southern state governments, with an unrecognized legal status, did not possess the resources to do the job, and it was too big for private charity. Only the government at Washington could deal with the situation.

The national government was in 1865 a more powerful and positive authority than ever before, but nothing in the American experience suggested that government had any obligation to extend mass relief or rehabilitate a distressed area. So Washington undertook only limited action. When Congress created the Freedmen's Bureau in March 1865 to assist blacks in making the transition to freedom, it also empowered the agency to issue rations to the former slaves and to loyal whites. The bureau, acting on a large scale and with compassion and good sense, distributed between 1865 and 1870 more than 21 million rations—of which 15.5 million went to blacks and the rest to needy whites, including former Confederates. One Southern observer wrote gratefully: "There is much in this that takes away the bitter sting. . . . Even crippled Confederate soldiers have their sacks filled and are fed."

THE South recovered from the effects of the war with relative rapidity and deceptive ease. Its greatest resource, the land, could not be destroyed. Some crops were harvested in 1865, and after that, progress was steady. The production of cotton, the big money staple, boomed. In 1859 the South had turned out 4,508,000 bales. That figure was almost reached again by 1870; by 1880 the total was 6,357,000 bales. At the same time industrial facilities experienced a mild expansion. The number of spindles in cotton mills jumped from 300,000 in 1860 to 533,000 in 1880. The rail system was rebuilt, and about 7,000 miles of new track was laid by 1879. But industrial growth, while promising, fell behind that of the nation as a whole. The South's railroad mileage dropped from 26 to 19 per cent of the national total, and its factories from 15 to 11.5 per cent.

Nor was agricultural rehabilitation so healthy or so forward as it seemed. The census showed the number of farms increasing from 549,000 to 1,252,000, but the rolls listed as farmers, and by inference as owners, many men who were tenants. The evidence is not absolutely clear but it seems to indicate that, despite some increase in small owners, the plantation system survived and that various areas saw a trend to even greater concentration in large holdings. Furthermore, the rate of farm growth was far below that of the rest of the country in the same period.

At first the plantation owners tried to work their lands by paying wages to workers, most of whom were blacks. But the wage system soon had to be abandoned because there was not enough cash to sustain it. Out of this situation, there developed the South's peculiar sharecrop and crop-lien system in which produce and labor took the place of money. It was a system with almost infinite variations. Usually the landlord rented a strip of land to a sharecropper, commonly a Negro, and furnished him with a house, a team, tools and seed. In return the cropper pledged a portion of his crop, one third to one half, to the landlord. A somewhat different arrangement prevailed with the share tenant, who was usually white. The tenant provided his own tools, team and the like, and consigned a smaller portion of his crop to the owner.

The system depended upon credit all along the line. The planter borrowed capital from a banker or merchant, giving a lien on his part of the crop as security. The sharecropper, in order to live until his crop was harvested, had to have credit from the country storekeeper, who also protected himself by demanding a lien. The country merchant in turn depended on credit from city wholesalers.

The complicated structure could function only if all the parts worked. Often they did not. A bad year could wipe out the planter or the merchant. The cropper, unused to the mechanics of credit, frequently found at the end of a year that he was in debt to one or both of his creditors. In its long-range effects, the system fastened a static and oppressive economy on the South.

A SONG OF RECONSTRUCTION: THE UNREPENTANT REBEL

The rancor of the war died hard, as this song illustrates. It was widely sung at Confederate reunions, to a tune called "Joe Bowers." The words are sometimes attributed to poet Innes Randolph, sometimes to artist Adalbert Volck.

Oh, I'm a good old rebel!
Now that's just what I am;
For this "Fair Land of Freedom
I do not care a damn.
I'm glad I fit against it,
I only wisht we'd won,
And I don't want no pardon
For nothin' what I've done.

I hates the Constitution,
This great Republic, too,
I hates the Freedman's Bureau,
In uniforms of blue;
I hates the nasty eagle
With all his brag and fuss,
But the lyin', thievin' Yankees,
I hates 'em wuss an' wuss.

I hates the Yankee nation,
And everything they do;
I hates the Declaration
Of Independence, too;
I hates the glorious Union,
'Tis dripping with our blood;
And I hates the striped banner,
I fit it all I could.

I can't take up my musket
And fight 'em now no mo';
But I ain't gonna love 'em,
And that is sartain sho';
And I don't want no pardon
For what I was and am;
And I won't be reconstructed,
And I don't care a damn.

The landlord, to protect himself, pressed the tenant to concentrate on a single money crop, usually cotton, to the detriment of diversified farming. The cropper was seldom able to lay aside enough cash to raise himself to the owner class. In the years after the war, the most salient fact about the South was that most of its people were pitifully poor. This poverty affected whites as well as blacks; it influenced subtly every white reaction to the politics of Reconstruction and race.

SOUTHERN whites, although not then aware of it, were part of a unique historical episode. The only Americans ever defeated in war, they were about to become the only Americans ever subjected to government imposed from the outside. The experience would profoundly affect their psychology—and North-South relationships—for generations.

Then and after, Southerners would talk much about the harshness of the punishment meted out by the victor. By ordinary American standards, the "peace" was indeed severe. It included military occupation, government by Northern officials and an attempted change in the race relations of the region. But judged in the perspective of history and of later conflicts, the occupation period was remarkably mild. The only Confederate official who suffered execution was Henry Wirz, who had commanded Andersonville Prison, where at least 12,000 Federal soldiers had died. Few Confederate officials were imprisoned and only one, Jefferson Davis, for any length of time. Outside the freeing of the slaves, there was no mass confiscation of property. And no real attack was ever made on the South's social system. The area emerged from Reconstruction with essentially the same class and race structure it had at the beginning.

The time span of Reconstruction differed from state to state. It began in 1867 with the imposition of Radical Reconstruction and it ended when the white-native-Democrats voted out the black-outsider-Republican governments. The dates for this latter process varied widely. The whites recovered control in Virginia, North Carolina and Georgia as early as 1870. They took back Alabama, Arkansas and Texas in 1874 and Mississippi in 1875. Only in Florida, South Carolina and Louisiana was the process delayed until 1877, the traditional date for the ending of the era.

The story of Reconstruction is almost always presented in terms of simple stereotypes, as a clash between good and evil. Actually Reconstruction was a terribly complex episode, invested with all kinds of complications and contradictions in both South and North. It is too tangled and tragic a period to be treated as melodrama.

The first step in Radical Reconstruction, and to its Republican architects the vital step, was to ensure that the blacks were registered as voters in the South. The registration took place in the spring and summer of 1867. Two organizations did much of the spadework. Most active and successful were agents of the Freedmen's Bureau, some of whom acted out of a sincere belief in Negro rights and some because they had political ambitions and hoped to garner a grateful vote. Almost as effective were the leaders of a frankly political association, the Loyal League, or Union League, a secret society of Northern origin whose members had to swear to uphold Republican principles.

When the registration was completed in the 10 former Confederate states

As spectators crowd the trees, the body of Henry Wirz, commander of the infamous prison at Andersonville, is lowered to the ground after his execution near the Capitol in 1865. With the North still aroused by atrocity propaganda, a military court steam-rollered Wirz's conviction, ignoring rules of evidence and hearing witnesses who had memorized testimony.

(Tennessee having already returned), the rolls showed 703,000 black voters and 627,000 white voters. An estimated 100,000 whites were either turned down by the registrars or simply stayed at home. In each state there was a Republican majority, and there was a majority of black registrants in five —Florida, Alabama, Louisiana, South Carolina and Mississippi—although only in the last three did the black population number 50 per cent or more of the population. It is evident from the registration figures that in the first phase of Reconstruction whites, almost as much as blacks, contributed to the Republican voting strength.

FROM the moment the Republican program of Negro suffrage was made public, all classes of Southern whites objected to it. But among the whites, there was a significant difference in intensity of feeling. In general the farmers, the middle class and the poor whites of the South were violently opposed to granting the blacks any substantial political rights. The reaction of these men was starkly racial. They believed that blacks were inferior beings and should be held in an inferior position. "There is at this day," wrote one Northern observer, "more prejudice against color among the middle and poorer classes . . . who owned few or no slaves—than among the planters who owned them by scores and hundreds. . . . As in Mississippi and Tennessee, the small farmers in the Alabama legislature were the bitterest negro-haters in that body."

The planters and businessmen, the upper classes in the Southern social structure, were also opposed to Negro suffrage, and also on the ground that the blacks were a separate and inferior race. But some of them, accustomed to directing blacks as slaves, thought that they could control them as voters. One plantation owner was quoted as saying that "the old owners would cast the votes of their people almost as absolutely and securely as they cast their own." This was precisely what many small farmers feared would happen

A uniformed agent of the Freedmen's Bureau stands as a symbol of peace between bands of white Southerners and the former slaves whom the bureau sought to rehabilitate. At first army officers served as bureau agents, but one general reported in vexation that most officers had "little or no interest" in black problems; some, it was said, were filled with race prejudice.

and was an added reason for their objection to Negro suffrage. One of them said of the planter: "He would be enabled to march to the polls with his two or three hundred 'freedmen' . . . voting as he directed, and control all elections. The poor white men . . . would have no influence."

But the most significant element in the upper-class reaction was its strong economic orientation. The rich whites disliked the idea of Negro suffrage partly for racial reasons, but primarily because it meant granting the vote to a propertyless class. In simplest terms, they feared that suffrage for the freedmen would lead to an attack on the interests of property. This apprehension, common to wealthy minorities in other 19th Century countries as well, was expressed in all the South but nowhere so completely as in New Orleans, the section's mercantile center. "Wherever voters greatly outnumber property holders, property will assuredly be unsafe," ran one typical comment. "Were universal negro suffrage to be added to the white universal suffrage now existing in the South, the security of both life and property would be greatly weakened. . . . The control of taxes must be left to those who pay them, and the protection of property to those who own it."

One journalist summed up in a revealing sentence the whole conservative concept of the importance of voting: "We look upon it as a duty rather than a right, and regret that there is so much of it among the whites."

The free black Pinckney Pinch-back was at one time the slave of a Mississippi River gambler who taught him every crooked trick of the trade. While his mentor fleeced passengers abovedeck, "Pinch" worked over the blacks below—appropriate training for his career as a corrupt Louisiana politician.

THE Republicans disregarded all these white attitudes and imposed Negro suffrage on the South in 1867. Thereafter, for varying periods in different states, the blacks became a potent political power, furnishing the bulk of the votes that sustained the Republican machines. They did not, however, receive offices in any ratio to their numbers, and they were almost uniformly denied the highest offices. In no state were they a majority in the legislature, although for a short time they controlled the lower house in South Carolina. No black was elected governor, and only in Mississippi, Louisiana and South Carolina did blacks become lieutenant governors. The Negroes' share of local offices was even smaller. Mississippi, where blacks outnumbered whites 437,400 to 353,800, had only one black mayor and 12 black sheriffs. On the national level, two blacks sat in the United States Senate, Hiram R. Revels and Blanche K. Bruce of Mississippi. During the entire Reconstruction period only 16 blacks were elected to the House of Representatives or the Senate, and only eight of these served at the same time.

Blacks who did hold office showed varied abilities and aspirations. Some were blatant professional politicians, interested only in power. Such a one was Pinckney Benton Stewart Pinchback, supposedly the son of a Mississippi planter and a slave woman who was emancipated by the father and sent to Ohio. Pinchback arrived in occupied Louisiana during the war and became the most powerful black in the state, serving as lieutenant governor and briefly as acting governor. But he never indicated that he saw Reconstruction as anything other than an opportunity for personal preferment for himself and other local politicians.

Of a different mold were the two senators, Revels and Bruce. Both were born in the South and went North while young men. Revels, a free black, was educated at Knox College, and Bruce, who attained freedom later in life, at Oberlin College. Appearing in Mississippi early in Reconstruction, they immediately took positions as leaders. They were sincerely intent on advancing

Blanche K. Bruce, the first black to serve a full term in the U.S. Senate, began life as the slave of a planter. Freed before the war, he attended Oberlin, acquired—as a contemporary later put it—"almost the manner of a Chesterfield," and returned to the South in 1868. By 1874 he too was a wealthy planter.

the rights of Negroes, but both also advocated the relaxation of disabilities on Confederates and hoped to work out means for whites and blacks to live together with mutual trust.

In many ways the most remarkable man among the black leaders was Dr. Louis C. Roudanez of Louisiana. A free Negro, wealthy and Paris-educated, Dr. Roudanez founded after the war the nation's first daily Negro newspaper, the New Orleans *Tribune*, and crusaded with idealistic fervor for land reform and equal distribution of property. With the same spirit he denounced the white Republican leaders for their lack of concern over black welfare, calling them "a petty clique of men . . . whose sole motive is greed."

WHITE men determined policy in all the state Republican organizations. There were two classes of white leaders: native Southerners, called "scalawags" (a popular term meaning runty or mean), and Northerners, or "carpetbaggers" (because supposedly they came South with just enough possessions to cram into a small bag). The scalawags were as influential as the carpetbaggers and occasionally more so. In the Mississippi constitutional convention, there were 17 blacks, 19 white Democrats, 26 carpetbaggers and 29 scalawags. The figures for Georgia are even more startling: 33 blacks, 12 white Democrats, nine carpetbaggers—and 116 scalawags.

In the mythology of Reconstruction the scalawag appears as an unscrupulous adventurer who crawled up out of the lowest levels of Southern society to seek power and pickings. Some scalawags fitted the description exactly, but most of them were upper-class whites—planters and businessmen who had opposed Negro suffrage primarily for economic reasons. Now that the black vote was an actuality, these men thought the realistic thing was to accept it. They believed that they could control the Negroes, and if they had to join the Republicans to do so, they had no objection. From the beginning scalawags were strongly ensconced in the seats of Republican power. Of the 76 most prominent Republican officeholders in Alabama between 1870 and 1875, seven were blacks, 24 were carpetbaggers and 45 were scalawags.

Some noted men became scalawags. Well-born Franklin Moses Jr. of South Carolina had raised the Confederate flag over captured Fort Sumter and later served as a Confederate colonel. Turning Republican, he won the governorship of his state. His administration was so corrupt that it shocked even his Republican colleagues.

Governor Joseph Brown, as an ardent states' righter, had led Georgia into secession. During the war, still as a states' righter, he opposed every attempt of the Richmond government to exercise centralized control of the military effort. After the war he became a leading Republican. When Republican rule was overthrown, he returned to the Democrats and for years was the boss of the state and a Democratic senator in Washington.

Moses and Brown conform in most respects to the popular image of the scalawag. But much more typical was James L. Alcorn of Mississippi. A wealthy planter and important political figure before the war, Alcorn became the first Republican governor of his state. He was a cold realist who accepted the new power of the Negro: "I propose to vote with him; to discuss political affairs with him; to sit, if need be, in political counsel with him; and from a platform acceptable alike to him, to me, and to you, to pluck our common liberty and our common prosperity out of the jaws of inevitable ruin."

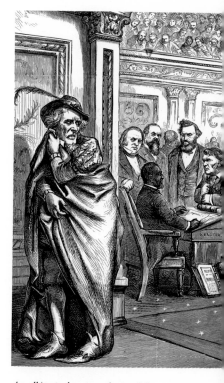

An allegorical cartoon depicts Jefferson Davis slinking away from the Senate, where black politician Hiram R. Revels occupies his seat. By 1876 sixteen blacks had served in Congress, and a Jackson, Mississippi, newspaper acknowledged: "They have shown consideration for the feelings of the whites."

133

The planter-businessman scalawags meant to manipulate the black vote for various ends. They wanted state aid to repair levees and construct railroads; they hoped to remove federal and state political disabilities on Confederate leaders; and above all they wanted to lighten the tax burden. The war had cut the value of Southern property by perhaps as much as half, and this depreciated total had to bear a tax rate that to those who had to pay it seemed confiscatory. To control the black vote the scalawags were willing to offer much—notably recognition of the Negroes' political and civil rights. Despite such concessions, they failed. Steadily and inevitably the scalawags lost their leadership to the carpetbaggers.

Former Union general Carl Schurz angered the Radicals by attacking carpetbaggers. But since Schurz himself had moved to Missouri and been elected to the Senate, Thomas Nast satirized him as the biggest carpetbagger of all. "The bag in front of him, filled with others' faults, he always sees," said Nast. "The one behind him, filled with his own faults, he never sees."

THE carpetbaggers were as varied a lot as the black and scalawag leaders. They had come South lured by the prospects of a society that seemed in revolution. Some wanted to reform that society on a progressive, Northern model. Characteristic of this type was Albion W. Tourgée of Ohio, who became influential in North Carolina. Although Tourgée was not oblivious to the rewards of politics, he was primarily concerned with social regeneration. Among other objectives, he labored to recast North Carolina's civil code along the lines of New York's.

In the end he had to admit failure; none of the people he had tried to uplift had wanted to be changed. He left North Carolina and wrote a semi-autobiographical novel, *A Fool's Errand*, in which he penned what might serve as an obituary for the hopes of the social reformers: "We tried to superimpose the idea of civilization, the idea of the North, upon the South at a moment's warning. We presumed that, by the suppression of rebellion, the Southern white man had become identical with the Caucasian of the North in thought and sentiment; and that the slave, by emancipation, had become a saint and a Solomon at once. . . . It was A FOOL'S ERRAND."

Some carpetbaggers who came South were moved by profound feelings of racial equality and justice. The most sensational of these was Albert Morgan from Wisconsin. He and his brother Charles tried to operate a leased plantation near Yazoo City, Mississippi, which they soon lost. Albert Morgan denounced his neighbors for their views on race relations and openly consorted with blacks. With their support he was elected state senator and then sheriff. The incumbent sheriff refused to yield the office and was killed in a gun battle between his followers and Morgan's. Morgan made an honest and energetic sheriff, but he had violated too many community standards ever to win the approval of the whites. Among other things, he had committed the unpardonable Southern sin—he married a beautiful quadroon schoolteacher from the North. Armed whites took possession of Yazoo City and Morgan had to leave the county in disguise.

Some carpetbaggers came for loot alone. A typical and engaging example was Milton S. Littlefield. An Illinois officer in the war, he set up headquarters in North Carolina in 1867, with a secondary base in Florida. He and his associates for years ran profitable deals that involved speculation in state bonds and state-supported railroads. For all the money he made, however, the likable and loud Littlefield was only a front man for native North Carolinians. He left the state near the end of Reconstruction and defied all attempts to extradite him to stand trial. There is a story that North Carolina finally sent an emissary to ask him to return voluntarily. Littlefield gave his visitor a set of documents to study and said the state would have to guarantee that all those involved with him would also have to be tried. The emissary read the papers and got the point. He said: "General, I respect your condition. I do not think we will trouble you any more."

Most typical of the carpetbaggers were those who came South solely to attain high political office. Many of them wanted power only for monetary and partisan rewards; such men generally returned North when Republican rule ended. Others, although not above exploiting political office for material gains, actually hoped to benefit the South, to bring about an adjustment in race relations, to improve the section's economy.

The outstanding carpetbagger of this type was Henry C. Warmoth from Illinois and Missouri, who became governor of Louisiana. A bold and imaginative operator, Warmoth established almost dictatorial authority over state and local government. A critic described him with unwilling admiration as "such a man as would rise to power in any great civil disturbance, embodying in himself the elements of revolution, and delighting in the exercise of his natural gifts in the midst of political excitement."

As a realistic politician, Warmoth felt he had to allow a measure of graft, and he took some himself. With the same realism, he saw that too much would hurt the party and the state, and he antagonized his followers by vetoing some corrupt bills. He also angered the blacks by vetoing a civil-rights bill that he considered too extreme. "We cannot hope by legislation," he said, "to control questions of personal association; much less can we hope to force on those who differ from us our views of what is humane, or courteous, or Christian-like." After Reconstruction, Warmoth remained in Louisiana and became a respected sugar planter. He died in New Orleans in 1931.

The carpetbaggers could seize Republican leadership from the scalawags for several reasons. Although the scalawags would concede the legal equality of blacks, they drew the line at social relationships. The carpetbaggers fixed no line. They ate, drank and danced with the blacks. They were ready to promise, if they did not always deliver, more of everything that the blacks wanted. They attracted the support of the professional black politicians (who commanded great influence with the black masses), though the more idealistic black leaders tended to distrust them.

ONE factor alone was sufficient to prevent a lasting alliance between the upper-class Southern whites and the blacks. The whites meant to use the black vote to reduce taxes. The blacks for their part demanded objectives that would cost much money. Reconstruction government was extremely expensive, and its tax burden fell on the propertied minority. The scalawags opposed the rising budgets. The carpetbaggers encouraged the rise.

The budgets spiraled to heights that seemed astronomical in comparison with the prewar figures. Louisiana's debt soared from $17,347,000 in 1868 to $29,619,000 in 1872, and Alabama's from $8,355,000 to $25,503,000. Taxes rose accordingly. In one Mississippi county in 1866, the rate was $3.25 on each $1,000 of property; eight years later it had climbed to $30.

Reconstruction government was expensive in part because it was corrupt. The dishonesty of the Republican regimes is a familiar story. In Florida the cost of official printing in 1869 exceeded the total expenditures of the state government in 1860. In Arkansas a black politician received $9,000 to repair

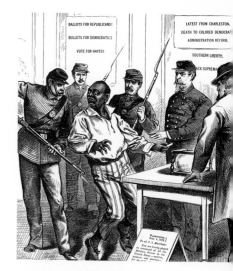

Loyal to Lincoln's memory, most blacks voted Republican. Nevertheless, as these cartoons of the 1876 elections show, the parties accused each other of intimidating black voters. Above, Federal troops are depicted helping a voter cast his ballot for the Republicans. Below, one white party worker tells another: "Of course he wants to vote the Democratic ticket!"

An 1867 cartoon shows former Rebel cavalryman Wade Hampton, still in cavalry boots and spurs and wearing a tattered plume in his hat (plus a cat-o'-nine-tails in his pocket), assuming his postwar role as politician. Seeking Negro support, he says to an ex-slave: "Of course you'll dine with me on Thursday?"

a bridge which had cost the state $500 to build. When the speaker of the South Carolina House lost $1,000 on a horse race, his colleagues voted him a $1,000 reward for his fine work as a presiding officer.

The corruption was wide and deep. But it must be placed in the setting of the time. It was not just the work of dishonest men, although there were plenty of these. Rather it was the product of profound forces that affected all parts of American society. After the idealism of the war came a kind of moral letdown. Material standards predominated, and people were not shocked at peculation in government. Corruption in Northern state and city governments exceeded anything in the South and touched even the national government. The chief corrupting agent was an expanding industrial capitalism. In a period of booming economic growth, everybody wanted quick results—businessmen, politicians and the people—and if the results had to be hurried with some purchased votes, what did it matter? This urge to expand affected Southerners as well as Northerners. The South needed capital to repair its shattered economy and was pathetically eager to secure industry. Every Southern state subscribed public credit to encourage railroad construction. The speculators who handled the railroad bills in the legislatures found they could buy Democratic votes quite as easily as Republican votes.

RECONSTRUCTION government was costly by its very nature. This was government of and for—if not always by—poor people, the first of its kind in American history. The Negro masses whose votes sustained the Republican organizations demanded a program of public works employment, poor relief and social services. In a vague way Reconstruction foreshadowed the later welfare state. The creation of the Freedmen's Bureau, for example, was a tacit recognition by the national government that it had an obligation to assume a welfare function. And when the bureau's agents sat in on negotiations of labor contracts between planters and field hands, the government was anticipating its modern role as a mediator in collective bargaining.

One of the major social demands advanced by the blacks was for increased public school appropriations. The desire of the Negro masses for education was real and insistent. As a result, for the first time Southern states provided something like adequate funds for the schools. South Carolina, which had 30,000 pupils in 1868, could boast 123,035 by 1876.

Although the blacks were the force behind the expanded school system, they were largely content to accept separate facilities. The constitutions of all the states expressed a general belief in equal education, but only two, Louisiana and South Carolina, specifically forbade segregated arrangements. Only in New Orleans did the Negroes and their Radical allies make a determined effort to mix the races in the schools. There at least 21 schools, about one third of the total, were integrated, and at one time an estimated 500 to 1,000 black pupils attended with whites.

Otherwise, however, there was little integration in any area of social life. The Negroes for the most part were satisfied to win recognition of their rights without attempting to exercise them. "We have no disposition to Africanize this state," one black leader assured Louisiana. "Let us be like the black and white keys of a piano, independent in their construction, but intended for combination, whose mutual reliance and association when blended together . . . compose an admirable and thrilling degree of musical perfection."

Just as there were blacks who would not push integration to the ultimate limits, there were whites who would accord the other race a large measure of civil rights. There had been no need for segregation under slavery. Therefore the pattern of segregation did not spring full-blown to the Southern mind at the beginning of Reconstruction. The white masses, who had violently opposed Negro suffrage, resisted with equal intensity any concession of social rights. But the upper-class whites, who had conceded on the suffrage, had a softer and more sophisticated view of race relations than the farmers. They could advocate compromise from a safer basis; their wealth meant they would not have to encounter the effects of integration in public transportation or public schools. Recognition of black civil rights was the bait held out by the rich whites in their last attempt to control Reconstruction.

As governor of Mississippi from 1869 to 1871, Southerner James L. Alcorn appointed a carpetbagger to the state's supreme court and backed a law intended to suppress the Ku-Klux Klan. But as a senator he later regained the esteem of his fellow Mississippians by opposing an integrated school system.

WHEN carpetbag leadership forced the scalawags out of the Republican party, these planter spokesmen did not immediately join the Democrats or abandon their hopes of securing the black vote. Instead they invited the Negroes to leave the Republicans and the carpetbaggers and affiliate with them in a new political organization distinct from the Democrats. The most elaborate and significant of these efforts was the Louisiana Unification Movement of 1873. Designed to combine the races in one great party that would end Reconstruction and restore economical government, the movement was headed by Louisiana's war hero General Beauregard. It attracted the support of practically the whole business community of New Orleans, of influential newspapers and of many planters in the southern section of the state. The Roman Catholic archbishop of New Orleans urged Catholics to give it their backing.

The unifiers held forth broad promises. They pledged full recognition of the civil and political rights of all citizens as guaranteed by the laws and the rules of "honor, brotherhood and fair dealing." They condemned segregation in "places of public resort" and in public conveyances. They asked for the admission of blacks to public schools on an equal basis with whites. They even recommended that black stockholders in corporations be accorded the privilege of sitting on boards of directors and that employers make no racial distinction in hiring.

Beauregard begged the whites to accept these concessions. But his plea did not move the white masses. They would not, for any ends, consent to even an abstract recognition of civil rights. The Shreveport *Times*, a leading segregationist newspaper, shouted: "The battle between the races for supremacy . . . must be fought out here . . . boldly and squarely; the issue cannot be satisfactorily adjusted by a repulsive commingling of antagonistic races." The unifiers did not arouse much enthusiasm even among the black masses. Some of the more idealistic black leaders adhered to the movement, but the professional black politicians, seeing in it a real threat to their own power, played a large part in killing it.

A master politician and financial wizard, Governor Joseph Brown of Georgia spent a short time in prison after Lee's surrender. But the experience did not burden him with compassion for his fellow inmates; he later made a fortune in mining and railroading—using convict labor he leased at seven cents a day.

The Louisiana unifiers failed and so did similar movements in other states. The planter-scalawags gradually drifted into the Democratic camp. Eventually in every state all classes of the whites would stand arrayed against Republican rule, and one by one the Republican governments would fall. They would be overthrown by political action, by violence, by economic pressure and, finally, because in 1876-1877 they became involved as pawns in a great power play in national politics.

Engine vs. Indian on the frontier

ON May 10, 1869, a hitherto obscure spot in the Utah wilderness—Promontory, 53 miles northwest of Ogden—attained a unique place in American history. There two railroad engines, the Central Pacific's *Jupiter* out of Sacramento and the Union Pacific's *No. 119* from Omaha, touched cowcatchers—"facing on a single track," wrote Bret Harte, "half a world behind each back." This odd confrontation marked the completion of the first transcontinental railroad, and the event was celebrated with appropriate symbolism. The final tie was of polished laurel wood, and a final spike of gold was driven into place by a silver-plated hammer. For the railroad was the harbinger of wealth for a neglected section of the United States—that vast prairie region between the Rockies and the Mississippi which for half a century had been called "The Great American Desert." In enriching the prairies the railroad assured the prosperity of the entire nation. "The construction of a country-wide transportation system," a historian wrote, "was, in sum, essential to the emergence of a modern America." As this new America emerged, an old one faded. The West of the Indians and seething herds of bison was on its way to legend.

THE BEGINNING OF AN ERA is toasted as the first coast-to-coast railroad line is completed at Promontory. The two construction crews, joined by 600 well-wishers, drank to the event in champagne and smashed the empty bottles against the boilers of the locomotives. The rest of the nation got news of the linkup via the telegraph wires which paralleled the rail lines.

THE END OF AN ERA finds a lone Indian listening in puzzlement to the strange hum of the telegraph wires that will help bring to a close the life he knows. Once the West was spanned by wires and rails, white men quickly took over the territory that had been allotted to the Indians. By 1885 all but a few Indians in the West were living on government reservations.

Men from across two oceans, working on the railroad

OF all the difficulties faced by the railroads in building the transcontinental line, none was more bothersome than the shortage of labor. Irish immigrants were enlisted in great numbers, and the Central Pacific imported 15,000 coolies from China. The Chinese worked in native costumes, drank gallons of tea and took daily baths, which amazed their fellow employees. But the coolies were respected for their dependability and capacity for hard work. Although the tracklaying progressed at an average rate of only two and a half miles a day, this was considered good going in the face of the hazards—rugged terrain, snowstorms, avalanches, bison stampedes and Indian attacks.

A CHINESE COOLIE removes rock from a tunnel in the High Sierras. Nitroglycerin, recently developed, was used in blasting; as a result, between 500 and 1,000 Chinese workers were killed.

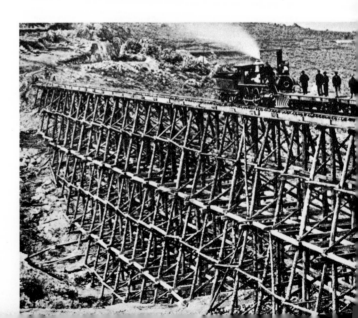

A CHAMPION CREW displays some of the equipment (*above*) that helped it lay 10 miles of track in a day. This feat won the Central Pacific's construction boss a $10,000 bet from an official of the Union Pacific. The U.P.'s best was eight and a half miles in one day.

A TEMPORARY TRESTLE, built in six weeks over a 450-foot cut east of Promontory, is crossed by Engine *No. 119*. The wooden trestles later had to be banked with rocks or replaced with a more durable construction. Promontory was bypassed by a new line in 1904.

End of the line for the bison

One of the West's last bison herds blocks a train's passage. A stampeding herd of buffalo, as they were always called, could actually knock over a train. The railroads hired hunters—Buffalo Bill Cody became the best known—to get rid of the menace. Later, hunting tours were organized and shooting bison

became a rich man's sport. But the slaughter of the animals reached its height—three million a year—between 1872 and 1874, after a Pennsylvania tannery began processing buffalo hides, for which it paid up to three dollars each. As bison vanished, the end of the nomadic Plains Indians became inevitable.

The animal's flesh was the Indians' principal source of meat; its skins provided clothes and tents. An 1889 census showed exactly 1,091 American bison left of the 12 million that had existed in the 1860s. As for the Indians, there had been a million in Columbus' time; by 1900 there were only 237,000 left.

A WAGON TRAIN, flanked by Custer's cavalrymen, winds through Castle Creek Valley during the 1874 Black Hills expedition.

BEAR HUNTERS show off a grizzly they shot in the Black Hills. At left is Bloody Knife, an Indian scout; Custer kneels in the center.

base near Bismarck, North Dakota, stands in snow-covered isolation on the Missouri. In 1895, with the Indian wars over, it was abandoned.

Gold strikes and Indian wars in the Black Hills

Aᴌᴛʜᴏᴜɢʜ suffering starvation, the Plains Indians had some hope for the future: by treaty with the United States they were allotted certain areas for their sole use. However, in 1874, Lieutenant Colonel George A. Custer, who had held general's rank in the Civil War, led an expedition into the Black Hills of the Dakotas, one of the Indian regions, presumably to seek a fort site. Instead, he found gold "from the grassroots down." In the gold rush which followed, prospectors clashed with Indians, U.S. troops were sent against the red men and the tribes were shattered. In these Indian wars Custer himself was killed in a famous massacre *(next page)*.

CUSTER'S NEMESIS, Sitting Bull *(right)* takes the sun outside his tepee with one of his several wives. He was a leader of the Sioux confederacy at the time of the Custer expedition.

145

Slaughter at Little Bighorn

Angered Indians attack an outnumbered force of cavalrymen under Custer in the battle at the Little Bighorn River in southern Montana in 1876. The fight resulted in the death of Custer's entire command, some 265 men. This painting, one of a number to depict "Custer's Last Stand," has several inaccuracies; for

example, Custer had actually cut his hair short, and he did not carry a sword. However, it does capture the fury of the conflict, which resulted from the refusal of the Indians led by Sitting Bull to remain on their reservations. Custer, a wily Indian fighter, acted here, it seems, foolhardily. He also underesti- mated the strength of his enemy—at least 1,000 fighting men, perhaps as many as 4,000. But this was a hollow victory for the Indians, and their last one. News of Custer's defeat so stirred the nation that the campaign against the Indians was stepped up. Someone later called the battle "The Indians' Last Stand."

7. THE POLITICS OF RECONSTRUCTION

O^N the night before the Republican convention met in Chicago in 1868, an association of Republican veterans held a gathering of their own. Among the dignitaries on the platform was Jesse Grant, father of the general who was slated to be the party's presidential nominee. The old man was called on to speak. As bands blared and the audience cheered, he rose and asked what he had done to be thus honored by "the braves of the nation." Back from the braves thundered the reply: "You had a son, that's enough."

When the regular convention assembled, the delegates could hardly wait for the nominations to be opened. John A. ("Black Jack") Logan, volunteer general in the Civil War, rose and said: "In the name of the loyal citizens and soldiers and sailors of this great republic, in the name of loyalty, liberty, humanity and justice, I nominate as candidate for the Chief Magistracy of this nation Ulysses S. Grant." The convention exploded in applause, and Grant was nominated unanimously on the first ballot. As vice-presidential candidate the Republicans chose Indiana's Schuyler Colfax. "His abilities are not distinguished," one leader confessed, "but are just sufficient to make him acceptable to the masses. They are fond of happy mediocrity."

It took the Republicans just two days in that cool May to transact their business. The Democrats wrangled through six hot July days in New York City before nominating Horatio Seymour, former governor of New York, slender and bald with an ear-to-ear beard that ran under his chin and made

A SOLDIER IN THE PRESIDENCY, U. S. Grant, first West Pointer in the office, is the image of probity in this painting, despite the scandals that tainted his Administration.

his face resemble "an outlined wriggle." Seymour charged that the Republicans had labored to create a centralized power and now had chosen "a military chieftain who stands at the head of that system of despotism which crushes beneath its feet the greatest principles of the Declaration of Independence." Second place went to Frank Blair Jr. of Missouri, a man of violent opinions who advocated that the President declare the Reconstruction Acts illegal and eject the carpetbag governments by force. About both the proceedings of the convention and its candidates there was an air of unreality.

Amid wild acclamation John A. Logan nominates Grant for President. Grant, a hero because of his Civil War record, had few qualifications for the presidency and, at first, little desire for the office. When a political delegation suggested in 1864 that he run for President, he retorted dryly: "I should like to be mayor of Galena." That was Grant's hometown in Illinois.

INDEED, there is to the modern reader a vague aura of unreality about the whole political scene in the postwar years. The struggles of the time seem like mock battles and the politicians like actors in some great farce. Yet the politics of Reconstruction had their own peculiar reality.

It was a transitional period in American politics, the end of one era and the beginning of another. The one issue that absorbed public attention was Reconstruction. Economic issues were stirring under the surface, but they were not yet dominant. Both the politicians and the people tended to back off from any fresh divisive issue; everybody remembered that the last time the country had faced up to a fundamental difference, a civil war had followed. As a result the two parties necessarily appeared much alike.

The Republican party was young, only a little more than a decade old, but to most Northerners its history was glorious. It was the party of Lincoln and the soldiers. It had emancipated the slaves and saved the nation. It stood for progress and the future. "I am a Republican," shouted Robert G. Ingersoll, the silver-voiced orator of the time, "because it is the only free party that ever existed. It is a party that has a platform as broad as humanity."

Just as the Republicans knew what their party was, they knew the Democratic party was the party of the South and slavery and treason. All Northern Democrats, it appeared from Republican campaign speeches, had secretly sympathized with the Confederacy and now were in league with Southern leaders to undo the results of the war. The Republican technique of recalling the emotions of the war was known as "waving the bloody shirt." The term originated when Benjamin F. Butler exhibited on the floor of the House a gory garment allegedly belonging to a carpetbagger who had been flogged in Mississippi. Ingersoll, also an enthusiastic shirt waver, once "wished there were words of pure hatred out of which I might construct sentences like serpents, sentences like snakes, sentences that would writhe and hiss—I could then give my opinion of the Northern allies of the Southern rebels."

This fervid oratory was in part a shrewd appeal to voter sentiment. The war's glories and sacrifices were still fresh in the public mind, and in identifying themselves with its results the Republicans were playing smart politics. But it was also a genuine expression of the idealism that had been such a large factor in the origin of Republicanism. The party had come into being as a representative of all the forces in Northern society opposed to slavery. Inevitably it had absorbed those economic elements which felt that Southern influence in the government denied them helpful legislation. From the start the Republicans had combined the idealism of antislavery and the material interests of Northern power groups.

But the party was slowly changing. It contained the same power groups: a manufacturing-financial wing based in the East but with growing branches in the West and an agricultural faction centered in the West. Both segments had secured legislative rewards during the war—in the way of tariffs, internal improvements and banking and land measures—and intended to retain them. Other important interest groups were the war veterans, perhaps a million of them, and the 703,000 Negro voters of the South, most of them Republican. The party continued to hand out awards to all these constituents. But the business and banking elements were gradually gaining an ascendant voice. At the same time, the earlier idealistic tone was disappearing among the leaders. By 1870 most of the old Radicals had died or retired. The new chiefs were men like Oliver P. Morton and Roscoe Conkling in the Senate and James G. Blaine and Ben Butler in the House. The Conklings and the Butlers might talk about ideals, but they were primarily interested in the political and economic spoils of power.

As for the Democrats, they were cursed by their past—not only by the immediate past of the war, but also by the distant past of their origin. They were committed to the Jeffersonian and Jacksonian philosophy that the national government should have as little power as possible and should not interfere with economic processes. That doctrine had served admirably in a simpler age. Now it prevented the Democrats from facing up to the problems of the new, postwar America. It restrained them even from representing adequately the groups that had always been their main support.

Historically the Democratic party had been the voice of the small man, of the average property holder and the farmer and the laborer. It contained a business wing of Easterners who represented financial and commercial interests, but this group was hardly dominant. Class consciousness was not strong in the immediate postwar period, but problems were emerging that would later inflame differences. Farmers and workers began to stir restlessly as business assumed a stronger role. The Democrats could have dealt with these problems only by advocating expanded national powers, which they could not bring themselves to do. On some economic questions they appeared as a "me too" party, quite as ready to please business as the Republicans.

THE economic issue that aroused the most dissension arose out of the currency situation. During the war the government had authorized the issue of $450 million in paper money as a temporary expedient to meet expenses. Under Johnson the Treasury had started to retire these "greenbacks," but so great was the protest that action had to be halted with $356 million in paper outstanding. Reactions to the greenback problem were so complex as to defy summary. In general, creditor and financial interests favored contraction or, in the phrase of the day, a return to the gold dollar. Debtor groups, mainly agrarian, advocated keeping the greenbacks and even increasing their amount. In 1868 some Western Democrats, seeking a good issue, moved toward inflation with the "Ohio Idea," which proposed that unless otherwise stipulated by law the bonds of the government should be paid in greenbacks.

The amorphous economic notions of the two parties appeared in the platforms they adopted in 1868. The Democrats accomplished a magnificent straddle on the tariff. They declared for "a tariff for revenue" that would also "promote and encourage" the industrial interests. On the money issue the Western Democrats succeeded in inserting an endorsement of the Ohio Idea. Candidate Seymour, a sound-money man, was so shocked at this departure

Horatio Seymour, 1868 Democratic candidate, swims helplessly in a "sea of troubles"—which is how he himself described his campaign. One of the most reluctant of U.S. candidates, Seymour disavowed all desire for the office five times. Only after he left the convention floor did the delegates nominate him unanimously. Then they adjourned before he could decline.

from orthodoxy that he indicated he would not abide by the currency plank if elected. The Republican platform called for the payment of the bonds in both the letter and the spirit of the laws contracting them, which was an indirect approval of gold. On the tariff question the Republicans took no stand whatsoever. With Seymour repudiating the greenbacks, there was thus no significant economic issue left in the campaign.

Both parties chose to emphasize Reconstruction. It was a natural issue for the Republicans, and they played it for all it was worth by endorsing the right of blacks to vote in the South. Unwisely, the Democrats met the challenge. They denounced the Reconstruction Acts as "unconstitutional, revolutionary, and void," implying that a Democratic President would throw them out by extralegal means. Such language made it easy for the Republicans to brand the Democrats as the allies of rebellion.

In the 1868 election the Republicans piled up an impressive electoral victory, 214 electoral votes to 80. Grant's popular vote, however, was only about 307,000 more than Seymour's. If, as is likely, upward of 450,000 black voters supported Grant, the surprising fact is that just three years after the war more white men preferred the Democratic candidate.

Later Grant would allude somewhat pathetically to his lack of background for the Presidency. "It was my fortune, or misfortune, to be called to the office of Chief Executive without any previous political training," he recalled in his last annual message to Congress. "From the age of seventeen I had never even witnessed the excitement attending a Presidential campaign but twice antecedent to my own candidacy, and at but one of them was I eligible as a voter. Under such circumstances it is but reasonable to suppose that errors of judgment must have occurred." Many of his mistakes, he continued, had been in giving important appointments to the wrong men. None of his failures could be laid to a bad intent. He had always tried to do the right thing.

Jay Gould, who almost created panic by attempting to corner the gold market, made a fortune by unscrupulous manipulation of railroads. "I don't build railroads; I buy them," he once said. He would loot a newly built line, sell out and use his profits to buy a parallel, competing railroad. Gould's former associates then had to agree to a merger and take a heavy loss.

GRANT'S confession constituted a concise history of his Administration and was not a bad self-portrait. Few men have entered the presidency under more difficult circumstances or with scantier qualifications for the office. The times called for a great professional politician, an Abraham Lincoln, a man who could sense what the public wanted and adjust to it but who could also mold and lead opinion. Grant's knowledge of politics, economics and government was elementary. He might have compensated by picking the right assistants. Instead he surrounded himself with mediocrities, incompetents and scoundrels. When the scoundrels were exposed for what they were, he refused to believe the evidence. Easily the most infamous of the inner White House circle was his private secretary, Orville Babcock, a gay, showy character who dominated the President's mind for eight years, destroyed Grant's confidence in good men, implanted his confidence in bad men—and held Grant's trust to the last.

Even if he had chosen able advisers, Grant could not have acted as a strong leader. He simply did not understand the American system of government or the role of the President. To him, Congress was the superior power and the function of the President was only to execute policy as determined by the legislative branch. In accepting the nomination Grant had said: "I shall have no policy of my own to enforce against the will of the people." He could not state his own views on any issues, he explained, because he did not know as yet the opinions of Congress. Grant would later dare to oppose Congress. But to the end he regarded the presidency as largely a ceremonial office.

Except for the greenback controversy (which was ultimately settled by an act providing for redemption of greenbacks with gold, effective in 1879), the economic issues of Grant's first term aroused little public attention. To the average voter such questions as taxes and tariffs were academic. Even more remote appeared another subject just beginning to be debated, civil service reform. The Reconstruction years witnessed a significant expansion in the number of government employees. In 1861 there were 36,672 workers, by 1871 the total had risen to 51,020 and by 1881 it would mount to 100,020. Some reformers contended that the increase in personnel made necessary a change to a merit method of selection. No longer could jobs be handed out as patronage awards, these men argued. Grant showed a slight interest in civil service reform but soon cooled off. American politics was not ready to be purified.

MUCH more intriguing to the public were two scandals that burst on the political scene during Grant's first term. The first of these began with a pair of the most daring and unscrupulous speculators in the country, James ("Jubilee Jim") Fisk Jr. and Jay Gould. Fisk was a loud, flashy character, a perfect model of the buccaneering capitalist, who amused himself with a private opera house and a private harem. Gould was a small, cold man, the schemer of the two. Having run up quick fortunes in railroad and greenback speculation, they now devised a plan breathtaking in its boldness—they would buy up all the gold offered for sale in the money market, hold it until the demands of trade forced the price up and then unload at a fabulous profit.

The scheme could succeed only if during the operation the Treasury did not release gold to the market. To assure Treasury cooperation, the two conspirators decided to draw Grant himself into the arrangement. They bought the services of Grant's brother-in-law, A. R. Corbin, and through him met the President socially, entertained him and gave him gifts. Into Grant's innocent ears they drummed one message—the sale of government gold in the months ahead would depress farm prices and damage Republican election prospects. Grant, always overly respectful of businessmen, seems to have given Fisk and Gould the impression that the Treasury would withhold gold.

In any event, convinced that they were protected, the pair began their operations in the summer of 1869. By September 22 they had driven the price of gold to astronomical heights, and on the 24th, "Black Friday," the whole financial community reached a state of panic. Not until then did Grant realize what was afoot. He finally ordered the Treasury to release gold, and the conspiracy abruptly collapsed. But hundreds of innocent investors had been ruined, and the President had been made to appear as the colleague of crooks.

The second scandal originated before Grant took office, but it was his bad luck to have it exposed during his Administration. During the Civil War the government had incorporated two companies, the Union Pacific and the Central Pacific, to construct a transcontinental railroad and had provided these concerns with generous financial assistance. To do the actual construction, the Union Pacific employed a company called the Crédit Mobilier—which, it later turned out, was secretly owned by stockholders of the Union Pacific who were out to milk their own company. The Crédit Mobilier received an estimated $73 million for work costing $50 million.

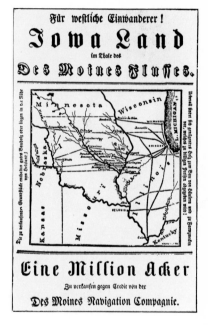

To entice land-hungry European peasants to settle on property near their lines, railroads distributed posters like this one offering Germans easy terms on a million acres of land in Iowa's Des Moines River valley. The high cost of wooing settlers away from competing railroads would be offset by the sizable profits from the freight traffic the newcomers would generate.

The promoters moved to stave off any federal investigation by selling Crédit Mobilier stock at a ridiculously low price to key members of Congress. But the arrangement became known. A congressional investigation disclosed that both Republicans and Democrats had accepted stock. More Republicans were involved, simply because Republicans were more valuable to the corrupters, and among them were some big names, including Vice President Colfax.

ALTHOUGH Grant was not directly involved in the scandals, many Republicans resented the whole direction the Administration was taking. Some were disgusted at the excesses and expense of Reconstruction and thought the time had come to end military rule in the South. Some objected to the President's failure to press tariff reductions. Still others condemned Grant's lack of vigor in pursuing civil service reform and his association with the ruthless party bosses, Conkling, Morton and Butler. By the election of 1872 the opposition to Grant had become so strong that his chief critics bolted the party and created their own organization, the Liberal Republican party. They meant to deny another term to Grant, who was assured of the regular nomination.

The rebels were a diverse set of men with discordant motives. Some were able and famous politicians: Senator Carl Schurz of Missouri; Senator Lyman Trumbull of Illinois, a veteran Republican who had voted against Johnson's impeachment; Justice David Davis of the Supreme Court, Lincoln's campaign manager in 1860; the cold, aristocratic Charles Francis Adams of Massachusetts, who had been minister to England during the Civil War. But essentially they were amateurs, intellectuals and editors: E. L. Godkin, editor of *The Nation* and an advocate of civil service reform; David A. Wells, who as Special Commissioner of the Revenue had vainly recommended tariff reduction; Horace Greeley of the influential New York *Tribune*, to whom a high tariff was almost an article of religious faith. The leadership illustrated the party's weakness. Not only was this an amateur party, but it represented practically every current economic view. The only unifying force was opposition to Grant.

The confusion of the Liberals was apparent when they met in convention at Cincinnati. With great difficulty they put together a platform. It approved the legislative fabric of Reconstruction but called for universal amnesty and withdrawal of troops from the South. It commended civil service reform and the redemption of the greenbacks. But on the tariff issue the convention split hopelessly. Unable to agree on anything, the delegates voted to refer the question to Congress and the people. The evasion augured ill for success in the election. The Liberals hoped to secure the endorsement of the Democrats and the support of the South; they would not get an enthusiastic response from either with this palpable dodge. They compounded the blunder by choosing Horace Greeley as their candidate.

Greeley, odd in appearance and manner, had almost every handicap known to politics. Millions of Americans who respected him as an editor and crusader viewed him personally as a colorful eccentric. In the course of his journalistic career of over 40 years, he had espoused all kinds of causes, including vegetarianism, spiritualism, land reform and antislavery. By committing himself on so many issues he had made many enemies. Notably he had offended Democrats and Southerners. Although he had spoken out against military Reconstruction and had gone bail for the imprisoned Jefferson Davis, he had also sneered that while not every Democrat was a horse thief, every horse thief was

"Panic, as a health officer," sweeps out of Wall Street the "garbage" of the 1873 financial collapse. Among the reckless speculators were members of Grant's Administration. Ex-President Andrew Johnson, impeached and almost convicted a few years earlier, could scarcely wait to get to Washington. To an immense crowd he gloated: "What kind of government have we now?"

a Democrat. The Democrats did endorse Greeley, but without enthusiasm.

The campaign turned into a venomous contest of abuse. Greeley denounced the corruption of the Grant Administration; the Republicans replied with pitiless attacks on Greeley's personality and record. The invective sickened Greeley. "I was assailed so bitterly," he said, "that I hardly knew whether I was running for the Presidency or the Penitentiary." In November Greeley went down to humiliating defeat, with 66 electoral votes to Grant's 286. Greeley was crushed; before the end of the month he was dead of what doctors diagnosed as "brain fever"—and, it may be suspected, of a broken heart.

Whatever the election portended—and it may have been no more than a rejection of a bizarre candidate—it appeared to indicate that the voters were not shocked by malfeasance in office. At least that seemed to be the lesson the politicians drew from the results. The second Grant Administration saw one dreary scandal after another. Secretary of the Treasury William A. Richardson and a special agent he appointed to collect delinquent taxes, John D. Sanborn, were exposed as the conductors of a profitable racket. Sanborn got a commission of 50 per cent on his collections, part of which went to party leaders. In one year he took as his share $213,500 and claimed he spent $156,000 as "expenses." Threatened by congressional censure, Richardson resigned—and was promptly elevated by Grant to a judgeship. Secretary of War William W. Belknap sold an Indian post-trader office; he resigned while impeachment proceedings were under way, but he too kept Grant's trust.

The most sensational scandal concerned the "Whiskey Ring," a gang of distillers and government officials who cheated the government of huge sums in taxes by filing false reports. When the new Secretary of the Treasury, Benjamin H. Bristow, prepared to bring the leaders of the ring to trial, Grant was properly virtuous. "Let no guilty man escape," he intoned. But it developed that his private secretary Babcock was involved. The President then insisted on making a written deposition for the good character of this favored scamp. Since Babcock could not be convicted without impugning Grant himself, the secretary was acquitted. Nor did the President stop here. He eventually forced Bristow, whom he blamed for persecuting poor Babcock, to resign.

Perhaps the voters were not shocked by the corruption in government because there was so much of it elsewhere. The disclosure of fraud after fraud in national, state and city affairs may have numbed the popular conscience. At the same time the country was reading about these Republican antics, it was treated to a juicy scandal that involved Tammany Hall, the Democratic machine that ruled New York City under William M. ("Boss") Tweed, a fat, ruthless organizer. Typical of the Tweed depredations was the construction of a courthouse for more than $11 million when the actual value was $3 million; one plasterer was paid $133,000 for two days' work, and the thermometers for the building cost $7,500. The total cost to the city of various Tweed Ring operations was estimated at $200 million over six years. Eventually Tweed was jailed and died in prison, but the power of Tammany was not seriously shaken.

Amidst all the bitter convulsion of Reconstruction, American foreign policy proceeded with comparative calm and unity. Spirited and even bold, it gave no hint of a nation troubled by domestic division. Lincoln's Secretary of State, William H. Seward, had continued in office under Andrew Johnson. An advocate of territorial expansion and a larger American role abroad, Seward

Horace Greeley, 1872 presidential candidate, was once fired because his boss wanted only "decent looking men in the office." As editor of the New York "Tribune," he wrote so illegibly that one reporter used a dismissal note from him as a recommendation. To even his anti-Grant backers, he was eccentric, but one claimed "a crooked stick" was needed "to beat a mad dog."

After eight years as Secretary of State under Lincoln and Johnson, William H. Seward made a trip around the world in 1870—first major American statesman to do so. One of his stops was Alaska, which he had bought for the U.S. in 1867 amid great controversy. This cartoon shows him with monogrammed bag, on his way to Alaska "to enjoy its genial climate."

had forced the French to abandon their puppet empire in Mexico, had engineered the purchase of Alaska from Russia for $7.2 million and had achieved the annexation of Midway Island in the Pacific.

One problem Seward was unable to settle. During the Civil War British shipyards had sold the Confederacy cruisers that had preyed on Northern commerce. After the war the United States had demanded payment from England for the damages committed by these ships. The most notorious raider had been the *Alabama*, and the demand became known as the "Alabama Claims." Seward negotiated an agreement calling for arbitration, but it was rejected by the Senate. Seward's successor, Hamilton Fish, continued to work for a solution. In 1871 the two governments agreed to the Treaty of Washington, a great landmark in the history of international arbitration. It provided for the submission of the cruiser issue and other disputes to international tribunals. These bodies awarded the United States $15.5 million for the Alabama Claims and England a total of $7,430,000 for certain counterclaims. The English-speaking nations had shown it was possible to settle serious differences without resort to force.

ET us have peace," Grant had written in 1868 in accepting the Republican nomination. He meant peace abroad and at home—and particularly in the reconstructed South. But peace in the South was one thing Grant would not enjoy. During his Administration Southern whites toppled one Republican state government after another from power. In some states the whites simply voted the Republicans out. Aiding the recovery process was the restoration of officeholding rights to those Southern leaders deprived under the 14th Amendment. Their number has been estimated at from 20,000 to 150,000 (it was probably nearer the first figure), but the general Amnesty Act of 1872 removed the disability from all but about 500.

The whites also resorted to intimidation to ensure their success. Secret societies sprang up all over the South to execute the white man's will. The most powerful were the Ku-Klux Klan and the Knights of the White Camelia. Both had elaborate rituals, and the members of both wore hooded and robed costumes. The ritual of the Knights of the White Camelia stated that "our main and fundamental object is the MAINTENANCE OF THE SUPREMACY OF THE WHITE RACE in this Republic."

Clad in their ghostly regalia, members would appear on horseback after dark at the homes of blacks. Stating in sepulchral tones that they were spirits from the other world, they would warn the residents to stay away from the polls. If this did not work, the night riders proved quite ready to flog, burn, drown and hang. They gave Republican officeholders a stipulated time period to clear out or suffer, in the words of one Klan missive, "retributive justice." Many of the recipients obeyed the hint. In 1870 the federal government began to act against these secret groups. Thousands of offenders were indicted, and although jury convictions were hard to secure, 1,284 were found guilty. By 1871 the Klan and the other orders had been so crippled that they never again were as important a political force.

Much more effective was another device the whites employed: semimilitary organizations that operated in open view. They went under various names— Rifle Clubs, Red Shirts, White Leagues—and their alleged purpose was to preserve law and order. The actual object was to overthrow Republican rule, if necessary by force. Their strategy was embodied in the phrase "drawing the color line." By legal or illegal means, every white man in a community would be forced to affiliate with the Democrats or leave. By similar methods every black would be driven from political life. The club members appeared, armed, at all elections, and they carried contest after contest for the Democrats.

The final weapon of the whites was the simple but terribly compelling force of economics. The war had freed the Negro, but he was still a laborer, a tenant or a hired worker. The Radicals had given him political power, but they had not given him the one thing he needed to sustain his power, a basis of economic security. Planters refused to rent land to Republican blacks; storekeepers refused to extend them credit; employers refused to hire them. The blacks might brave the Rifle Clubs, but they could not fight economic pressure.

By 1876 the whites had recovered control in every state except South Carolina, Florida and Louisiana. Reconstruction was drawing to a close—and that year's election finished the process.

The Democrats in 1876 were buoyed by visions of victory. Two years earlier they had captured control of the House for the first time since 1858. They believed the country was tired at last of corruption, and their candidate seemed to embody perfectly the national mood. He was Samuel J. Tilden, who as governor of New York had made his name synonymous with reform and economy. The Republicans nominated Rutherford B. Hayes, a man of solid reputation, three times governor of Ohio and an advocate of civil service reform.

THE results of the election were fiercely disputed. Both parties claimed the 19 electoral votes of the three Southern states still in Republican hands—and these votes would be decisive. The country faced the prospect of having no President in March. Across the land there was ugly talk of violence, and President Grant warned that any "warlike concentration of men" would be met by the invocation of martial law.

At the height of the crisis sectional leaders of both parties entered into some complicated bargaining. The outcome was that the disputed votes and the presidency were awarded to Hayes—just two days before the inauguration date. The Southern Democrats had consummated one of the most amazing deals in political annals.

It was said at the time that the Southerners had exacted as the price of their support a pledge that Hayes would withdraw the remaining federal troops from the South. The story seemed plausible. After he became President, Hayes did remove the troops, the last Republican governments fell and Reconstruction came to an end.

Americans reacted to the purchase of Alaska with cries of "Seward's Folly." In a cartoon of the day, Brother Jonathan (an ancestor of Uncle Sam) pays $7.2 million for what the caption called "a purty big lump of ice." The picture below shows Seward and President Johnson inviting an Eskimo and what was described as a "seal" to dinner. The caption: "Our New Senators."

But actually, as the Southerners knew, Hayes, a conservative, was probably going to take the army out anyway; they demanded and got the promise of greater concessions—federal subsidies for a Southern transcontinental railroad, federal assistance for other internal improvements and control of federal patronage in the region. But they could not have explained all this to their people without the symbol of the departure of the troops.

There was a much greater symbol in the Compromise of 1877. After many ordeals—sectional controversy, Civil War, Reconstruction—the American people had renounced force as a method of settling their domestic disputes. It was the most lasting compromise in American history. The Union was now fully and finally restored.

FREEDOM'S TORCH, part of F. A. Barthol-
di's Statue of Liberty, juts up outlandishly
at the Centennial Exposition in Philadelphia, where it was shown before the
statue was erected in New York Harbor.
In the 1870s, immigration, later symbol-
ized by this statue, reached a new high.

A vigorous nation at its centennial

IN 1876 the United States celebrated its centennial year with a great exposition in Philadelphia. Stirred by the anniversary, Americans everywhere
paused for a proud backward look. Their first century as a nation had been
one of epic growth and achievement. America's 13 states had grown to 38, its
population (including more and more immigrants) from 2.5 million to 46 million, its area from 889,000 square miles to three million. Through individual
enterprise, a vast prehistoric wilderness had been turned into a productive
rural landscape, and bustling cities now stood where unlettered tribesmen
had recently built their campfires.

The nation's greatest progress, as the Philadelphia fair demonstrated in
spectacular modern displays, had come in the decade just past. A combination of science and the machine had repaired much of the desolation of the
Civil War, had riveted the nation together with an ever-widening network
of rails, and had converted an incalculable treasure of raw materials into a
colossal flood of manufactures. It was this vigorous decade, and the easier life
it produced, that put on U.S. civilization the stamp it has borne ever since.

AMERICA'S BIRTHDAY is celebrated in 1876 with appropriate ceremony. Milling around the speakers' platform
are vendors, children, and women in their Sunday best.

NEW ARRIVALS gather in a New York immigration depot awaiting admittance to "The Land of Promise." With the rise of immigration, by 1875 almost one fifth of the U.S. population was foreign-born.

NEW RESIDENCES for teeming New York are started by workers excavating along 46th Street, east of the Lexington Avenue Presbyterian Church (center background), in 1868.

American cities in a turmoil of expansion

IN the tremendous postwar industrial boom, America's cities grew at an explosive rate. Their populations were swollen by immigrants *(opposite)*; 250,000 arrived in 1865, some 460,000 in 1873—nearly 3.5 million all told in the decade ending in 1875. By 1870 Philadelphia with almost 750,000 inhabitants and Chicago with 300,000 were reeling under the crush.

But it was New York, whose population passed one million by 1875, that suffered the worst of urban growing pains. Great traffic jams snarled business in the old downtown section. Stepped-up construction *(below)* failed to meet the need for new housing. Shantytowns sprawled along the rivers and foul tenements encroached on fine Broadway stores and Fifth Avenue mansions. New York, said a visitor, was "a lady in ball costume, with diamonds in her ears and her toes out at her boots."

A prosperous country town, its main street winding through a crenelated covered bridge (right) and past a paper mill (left), nestles in

A rich wheat harvest is brought home in California. The success of grain-growing here and in the prairie lands helped increase the farm

the fertile hills of Pennsylvania. In the 1870s the inhabitants of such rural communities outnumbered city dwellers in all but five states.

population of these regions by about 1.5 million during the 1870s.

The new attractions
of the rural life

Iᴺ spite of the phenomenal growth of cities, fully three quarters of the U.S. population in the 1870s lived on farms or in small country towns that subsisted chiefly on agriculture. But farming, too, was changing with the times. Vast new tracts fell to the plow and were planted to grain *(left)*. Crops were harvested by more and better farm machinery. Scientific methods were spreading. As production increased, its proceeds permitted many work-worn farmers to enjoy for the first time certain comforts of life; and "clean, bright, gardened townships" sprang up, promising "country fare and pleasant summer evenings on the stoop."

163

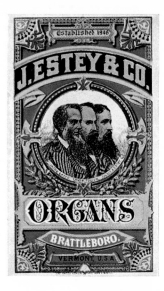

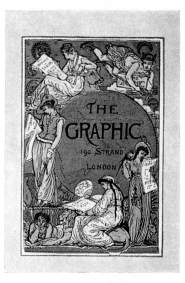

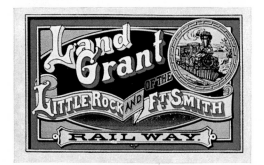

Manufacturers' trade cards, handed to visitors, advertise a wide range of products and services exhibited or promoted at the exposition.

164

More than 100,000 hardy visitors watch in the rain as the Centennial Exposition is opened with ceremonies in front of the Main Building.

A wondrous display
of the nation's ingenuity

IN Philadelphia's Fairmount Park on May 10, 1876, President Grant officiated at the opening of the great exposition that celebrated the nation's centennial year. In spite of bad weather and the high cost of travel, huge crowds came—up to 274,000 a day. They saw countless exotic displays sent by foreign countries: stuffed crocodiles from Egypt, a model pagoda from China, beehives from England. Each of the 38 states had exhibits, usually of such homely items as apples from Nebraska and nuts from Oregon. But in these aggressively modern times, machines and inventions were by far the most popular of all the exhibits. The men marveled at a calculating machine that fit into only 15 square feet of space, and they took special satisfaction in the American manufacture of the most powerful engine built to date *(right)*. The ladies buzzed around a spectacular array of sewing machines, while the youngsters admired several newfangled soda fountains. Among the displays was Alexander Graham Bell's first telephone. When Emperor Dom Pedro of Brazil put its receiver to his ear, he exclaimed in awe, "My God! It talks!"

MOST POWERFUL MACHINE of its day, the Corliss Engine generated up to 2,500 horsepower—and tremendous vibrations. George M. Pullman later bought it for his sleeper-car factory.

165

Visible reason for hope

In their stylish carriages visitors depart the exposition, whose main buildings can be seen at right center, and prepare to return to Philadelphia across the Schuylkill River. By the time the great fair closed in November 1876 almost 10 million Americans had examined its exhibits, leaving with a sense of pride

in their country's past and high expectations for its future.

Indeed, the U.S. had cause for optimism. The worst wounds of the Civil War had healed; even the Southern states were backing the increase of federal powers. *The Nation's* editor Edwin Godkin summed up what was, perhaps, the century's greatest achievement. Americans themselves, he said, "are far less raw and provincial than their fathers; they have seen more, they have read more, they have mixed more with people of other nationalities, they have thought more and had to think more, they have spent more for ideas and given more away."

CHRONOLOGY   *A timetable of American and world events: 1861-1876*
(The narrative account of Civil War political events listed below appears in Volume 5)

WORLD EVENTS	EXPANSION and EXPLORATION	POLITICS	MILITARY	ECONOMICS and SCIENCE	THOUGHT and CULTURE
1861 Czar Alexander's Emancipation Edict frees Russian serfs	1861 Kansas statehood	Jan.-Feb. 1861 Mississippi, Florida, Alabama, Georgia, Louisiana and Texas join South Carolina in seceding from the Union	April 1861 Confederates fire on Fort Sumter	1861 Morrill Tariff raises duties generally, with low-tariff Southerners no longer in Congress	1861 Yale awards first Doctor of Philosophy degree granted in U.S.
1861 Kingdom of Italy is formed with Victor Emmanuel as king	1861 Colorado, Nevada and Dakota territories organized	Feb. 1861 Delegates of seven seceding states, meeting at Montgomery, Alabama, draft Confederate Constitution, elect Jefferson Davis President	April 1861 Lincoln calls for 75,000 volunteers and orders naval blockade	1861 Confederacy issues first bank notes	1861 Winslow Homer joins McClellan's army as special artist for *Harper's Weekly*
1861 Prince Albert of Britain dies	1861 Telegraph lines link East and West Coasts	March 1861 Abraham Lincoln inaugurated President	July 1861 First Bull Run	1861 Dorothea Dix appointed superintendent of women nurses for Union army	1862 Publication of Julia Ward Howe's "Battle Hymn of the Republic"
1861 Mexico invaded by European forces		April-May 1861 Virginia, Arkansas, Tennessee and North Carolina secede	August 1861 Battle of Wilson's Creek, Missouri	1862 First issue of greenbacks	1862 Morrill Land Grant Act provides federal aid for states to endow agricultural and technical colleges
1861-76 Abdul Aziz reigns in Ottoman Empire		June 1861 West Virginia breaks away from Virginia, remains loyal to Union	Nov. 1861 Confederate commissioners removed from British ship *Trent*	1862 Department of Agriculture established	
1861-88 William I reigns in Prussia		August 1861-July 1862 Confiscation Acts lay groundwork for freeing of slaves	Feb. 1862 General Grant and Commodore Foote capture Forts Henry and Donelson	1862 First federal income tax	
1861-89 Louis I rules Portugal		April 1862 Slavery abolished in the District of Columbia	March 1862 Federal victory at Pea Ridge	1862 Richard J. Gatling perfects the revolving machine gun	
1862 Slavery abolished in Dutch West Indies	1862 Great Sioux uprising in Minnesota	Sept. 1862 President Lincoln issues Emancipation Proclamation, to take effect Jan. 1, 1863	March 1862 Battle between ironclads *Monitor* and *Merrimack* at Hampton Roads, Virginia	1862 Jay Cooke floats large Civil War loan using patriotic appeals and advertising techniques	
1862-90 Otto von Bismarck serves as premier of Prussia and, later, chancellor of the German Empire	1862 Homestead Act		March-June 1862 Jackson's Shenandoah Campaign	1862 "Molly Maguires," members of secret organization of miners, begin operations in eastern Pennsylvania	
			April 1862 Confederate Conscription Act		
			April 1862 Battle of Shiloh		
			April 1862 Occupation of New Orleans		
			April-July 1862 Peninsular Campaign		
			August 1862 Second Bull Run		
			Sept. 1862 Lee's first invasion of the North; battle of Antietam		
			Dec. 1862 Battle of Fredericksburg		
			Dec. 1862-Jan. 1863 Battle of Murfreesboro		

1863 The War's Turning Points

WORLD EVENTS	EXPANSION and EXPLORATION	POLITICS	MILITARY	ECONOMICS and SCIENCE	THOUGHT and CULTURE
1863 International Committee of the Red Cross is organized	1863 West Virginia statehood	July 1863 Draft riots in New York City	March 1863 Union Conscription Act	1863 Confederate Congress enacts general internal revenue act	1863 Edward Everett Hale's "The Man Without a Country" published
1863 French troops occupy Mexico City	1863 Arizona and Idaho territories organized	Dec. 1863 Lincoln announces his plan for Reconstruction of seceding states	May 1863 Battle of Chancellorsville; death of Stonewall Jackson	1863 U.S. Congress gives land grant to Atchison, Topeka and Santa Fe Railroad	1865 *The Nation* begins publication with E. L. Godkin as editor
1863 French establish protectorate over Cambodia	1863 Gold rush in Montana	June 1864 Senate refuses to seat members from Arkansas, Tennessee and Louisiana seeking entrance under Lincoln Reconstruction Plan	July 1863 Lee's second invasion of the North; battle of Gettysburg	1863 Free-carrier mail service, providing first door-to-door delivery, authorized	1865 Vassar Female College opens
1863-64 Polish revolution against Russia suppressed		July 1864 Lincoln pocket-vetoes Wade-Davis bill for Radical Reconstruction of South	July 1863 Fall of Vicksburg	1863 Locomotive engineers organize successful railroad union	1865 Mark Twain's short story, "The Celebrated Jumping Frog of Calaveras County," published
1863-79 Ismail Pasha reigns as khedive of Egypt	1864 Militia massacres Indians at Sand Creek, Colorado	Nov. 1864 Lincoln re-elected President over McClellan	July 1863 Capture of Port Hudson, Louisiana	1864 Railway mail service begins	1865 Mary Mapes Dodge's *Hans Brinker; or the Silver Skates* published
1863-1906 Christian IX rules in Denmark	1864 Nevada statehood	1864-73 Salmon P. Chase serves as Chief Justice of U.S.	Sept. 1863 Battle of Chickamauga	1865 George Pullman builds "Pioneer," specially constructed sleeping car	
1863-1913 George I reigns in Greece	1864 Montana territory organized	March 1865 Freedmen's Bureau established	Sept. 1863 British bar delivery of British-built warships to Rebels; French follow suit	1865 Thaddeus Lowe invents a machine to make artificial ice	
1864 Maximilian is crowned emperor of Mexico	1864 Homestead Bonus bill for soldiers enacted	April 1865 Lincoln assassinated by John Wilkes Booth; Andrew Johnson takes oath as President	Nov. 1863 Battle of Chattanooga	1865 Congress imposes a tax on state bank notes; hundreds of state banks forced to become national banks, thus bringing about a uniform currency	
1864 The First Communist International is organized in London by Karl Marx		May-July 1865 Johnson puts his own Reconstruction plan into effect	March 1864 Grant takes supreme command	1865 First oil pipeline completed from Mills Farm, Pennsylvania, to Pithole, Pennsylvania	
1864 Prussia, Austria war with Denmark over Schleswig and Holstein		Nov. 1865 First "Black Code" enacted by Mississippi	May-June 1864 Confederate advance on Richmond	1866 Massachusetts enacts law barring children under 10 from factory employment	
1864-89 Protestant missionaries introduce Western ideas to China		Dec. 1865 13th Amendment, abolishing slavery, becomes effective	June 1864 Confederate raider *Alabama* sunk by U.S.S. *Kearsage* off Cherbourg, France	1866 Cyrus Field lays first successful Atlantic cable	
		April 1866 Congress overrides Johnson's veto of Civil Rights bill	June 1864-April 1865 Siege of Petersburg		
		June 1866 Committee on Reconstruction proposes congressional supervision of Reconstruction	August 1864 Battle of Mobile Bay		
			Sept. 1864 Sherman occupies Atlanta		
			Nov. 1864 Battle of Franklin		
			Nov.-Dec. 1864 Sherman's march to the sea		
			Dec. 1864 Battle of Nashville		
			Jan. 1865 Union forces capture Fort Fisher, North Carolina		
			Jan.-March 1865 Sherman's march through the Carolinas		
			March 1865 Confederate Congress approves military service for slaves		
			April 1865 Lee surrenders to Grant		
			April 1865 Johnston surrenders to Sherman		

1866 The Massachusetts Institute of Technology inaugurates the nation's first architecture courses

1867 *Harper's Bazaar* begins publication

1867 First running of the Belmont Stakes

1868 New York Athletic Club holds first track and field meet for amateur athletes in U.S.

1868 Publication of Louisa May Alcott's *Little Women*

1868 Susan B. Anthony founds the suffragette newspaper *The Revolution*

1866 National Labor Union, first organization of unions, established at Baltimore

1866-76 Wholesale price index for farm products declines 36.4 per cent

1866-1900 U.S. exports treble; imports double

1867 Patrons of Husbandry, later known as the Grangers, organized to promote farmers' interests

1868 Christopher Sholes patents the first commercial typewriter

1868 Congress approves first federal legislation for an eight-hour day, confined to laborers and mechanics in government employ

---

May 1865 General Richard Taylor surrenders, ending resistance east of the Mississippi

May 1865 Jefferson Davis captured

May 1865 General E. Kirby Smith surrenders, ending organized resistance

---

July 1866 New Freedmen's Bureau bill passed over Johnson's veto

July 1866 Tennessee is readmitted to the Union

Dec. 1866 Supreme Court, in *ex parte Milligan*, rules that martial law is unconstitutional where civil courts are in operation

1866 Ku-Klux Klan organized at Pulaski, Tennessee

March 1867 Congress enacts Command of the Army Act and Tenure of Office Act, sharply limiting presidential authority

March-July 1867 Three Reconstruction acts passed, dividing the South into military districts and setting up rigid new procedures for restoration of states

Feb. 1868 President Johnson removes Secretary of War Stanton without Senate approval

Feb.-May 1868 President Johnson is impeached, tried and acquitted

June 1868 Arkansas, Alabama, Florida, Louisiana, South Carolina and North Carolina are readmitted to the Union

July 1868 14th Amendment, granting Negroes citizenship, ratified

Nov. 1868 Ulysses S. Grant elected President

1866 "Long Drive" of cattle begins from Texas to Kansas and Nebraska railroad centers

1866 Five Civilized Tribes forced to cede half of present-day Oklahoma to the U.S. government

1867 Secretary of State Seward purchases Alaska from Russia for $7.2 million

1867 U.S. occupies Midway Island in the Pacific

1867 Nebraska statehood

1868 Wyoming territory organized

1865 Gregor Mendel, Austrian monk, describes the laws of heredity

1865 Lewis Carroll's *Alice's Adventures in Wonderland* is published

1865 Joseph Lister, an English physician, introduces antiseptic surgery

1865-1909 Leopold II reigns in Belgium

1867 Maximilian capitulates to Mexican rebels; Juárez elected president

1867 British grant dominion status to Canada

1867 Shogun Keiki resigns, ending centuries of feudal military rule in Japan

1867 Vast fields of diamonds discovered near Hope Town, South Africa

1867 North German Confederation organized

1868-74 William Gladstone serves as Britain's prime minister

1869 By Rail to the Pacific

1869 First intercollegiate football game, between Rutgers and Princeton

1870 *Scribner's Monthly* begins publication

1871 Great Chicago fire

1872 James McNeill Whistler's famed portrait of his mother first shown at the Louvre

1873 First U.S. performance of Verdi's *Aida*

1875 Smith College opens

1875 Publication of Mary Baker Eddy's Christian Science study, *Science and Health*

1875 Archbishop John McCloskey is named first American cardinal

1876 Baseball's National League founded

1876 Publication of Mark Twain's *Tom Sawyer*

1869 George Westinghouse patents the air brake

1869 Fisk-Gould scheme to corner U.S. gold supply fails

1870 Census shows population of 39,818,000, a 20.6 per cent increase since 1860

1872 Tariff of 1872 enacted, aimed at reversing protectionist trend

1873 Coinage Act demonetizes silver and makes gold the sole monetary standard

1873 Record-breaking 459,803 immigrants enter U.S.

1873-78 Depression triggered by the Panic of 1873

1874-76 U.S. experiences the worst grasshopper plague in its history

1875 Resumption Act provides that Treasury will redeem paper money in gold after January 1879

1875 Tariff of 1875 restores most earlier cuts in duties

1876 Alexander Graham Bell patents the telephone

1869 Nathan Bedford Forrest, Grand Wizard, orders the Ku-Klux Klan to disband

Dec. 1869 Wyoming passes first U.S. woman-suffrage law

Jan.-July 1870 Virginia, Mississippi, Texas, Georgia readmitted to the Union

March 1870 15th Amendment, giving Negroes the vote, ratified

July 1871 New York *Times* begins exposé of Tammany Hall corruption leading to eventual imprisonment of Boss Tweed

May 1872 General Amnesty Act permits all but some 500 Southern leaders to hold office

Sept. 1872 New York *Sun* charges prominent Republicans with taking bribes in Crédit Mobilier scandal

Nov. 1872 Grant re-elected President

March 1876 Secretary of War William W. Belknap, charged with selling an Indian post-tradership, resigns

Nov. 1876 Disputed presidential election contest between Samuel Tilden and Rutherford B. Hayes

---

1869 Congress creates Board of Indian Commissioners to supervise federal spending for tribes

1869 Transcontinental railroad completed

1874 Lt. Col. George Custer leads expedition to Black Hills and brings back reports of gold

1874 Boom in Dakotas settlement

1875 Sioux War begins

1876 Custer and some 265 men wiped out at Little Bighorn, Montana

1876 Colorado statehood

1876-77 Sioux War ends with defeat of Sitting Bull and Crazy Horse

---

1869 By Rail to the Pacific

1869 Suez Canal opens

1869-70 Vatican Council, first general council since 1563

1870-71 Franco-Prussian War results in French defeat

1871 Third French Republic is proclaimed

1871 William I of Prussia is crowned emperor of Germany at Versailles

1872-1905 Oscar II rules Sweden and Norway

1873-74 First Spanish Republic is organized

1874-80 Benjamin Disraeli serves as Britain's prime minister

1875 Balkan subject people revolt against Turks

1875 Britain purchases controlling shares of the Suez Canal

1876-1909 Abdul Hamid II reigns as Ottoman emperor

1876-1911 Porfirio Díaz rules as dictator of Mexico

FOR FURTHER READING

These books were selected for their interest and authority in the preparation of this volume, and for their usefulness to readers seeking additional information on specific points. An asterisk (*) marks works available in both hard-cover and paperback editions; a dagger (†) indicates availability only in paperback. Books dealing with the politics of the Civil War period are listed in Volume 5.

GENERAL READING

*Basler, Roy P. (ed.), *The Collected Works of Abraham Lincoln* (9 vols.). Rutgers University Press, 1953.

Boatner, Mark M. III, *Civil War Dictionary*. David McKay, 1959.

Carman, H. J., H. C. Syrett and B. W. Wishy, *A History of the American People* (Vol. II). Knopf, 1960.

*Commager, Henry Steele, *Documents of American History*. Appleton-Century-Crofts, 1963.

Davidson, Marshall, *Life in America* (2 vols.). Houghton Mifflin, 1951.

*Degler, Carl, *Out of our Past*. Harper & Row, 1958.

Hicks, John D., *Federal Union: A History of the United States to 1877*. Houghton Mifflin, 1952.

Hofstadter, R. W. Miller, and D. Aaron, *The American Republic* (Vol. II). Prentice-Hall, 1959.

Malone, Dumas, and Basil Rauch, *Empire for Liberty* (Vol. I). Appleton-Century-Crofts, 1960.

Morison, Samuel Eliot, and Henry Steele Commager, *The Growth of the American Republic* (Vol. II). Oxford University Press, 1962.

Nevins, Allan, *The War for the Union* (2 vols.). Scribner's, 1959-60.

Randall, J. G., and David Donald, *The Divided Union*. Little, Brown, 1961.

THE STRATEGY OF THE WAR (CHAPTER 1)

*Catton, Bruce, *Mr. Lincoln's Army*. Doubleday, 1951.

Coulter, E. Merton, *The Confederate States of America*. Louisiana State University Press, 1950.

Donald, David (ed.), *Divided We Fought: A Pictorial History of the War: 1861-1865*. Macmillan, 1952.

*Donald, David, *Lincoln Reconsidered*. Knopf, 1956.

*Eaton, Clement, *History of the Southern Confederacy*. Macmillan, 1954.

Foote, Shelby, *The Civil War: A Narrative*. Random House, 1958.

Freeman, Douglas S., *Robert E. Lee* (4 vols.). Scribner's, 1935.

Fuller, J.F.C., *Grant and Lee: A Study in Personality and Generalship*. Indiana University Press, 1957.

*Goodrich, Lloyd, *Winslow Homer*. George Braziller, 1959.

†Jones, John B., *Rebel War Clerk's Diary*. A. S. Barnes.

*Wiley, Bell Irvin, *The Life of Billy Yank* and *The Life of Johnny Reb*. Bobbs-Merrill. Also in one volume, *The Common Soldier in the Civil War*. Grosset & Dunlap, 1958.

ON THE BATTLEFIELDS (CHAPTERS 2, 3, 4)

Angle, P. M., and E. S. Miers, *Tragic Years: 1860-1865* (2 vols.). Simon and Schuster, 1960.

Catton, Bruce (ed.), *American Heritage Picture History of the Civil War*. Doubleday, 1960.

Catton, Bruce, *Grant Moves South*. Little, Brown, 1960.

*Catton, Bruce, *This Hallowed Ground: The Story of the Union Side of the Civil War*. Doubleday, 1956.

Commager, Henry Steele, *The Blue and the Gray*. Bobbs-Merrill, 1954.

Dowdey, Clifford, *The Land They Fought For: The South as the Confederacy 1832-1865*. Doubleday, 1955.

Freeman, Douglas S., *Lee's Lieutenants* (3 vols.). Scribner's, 1942-44.

†Grant, Ulysses S., *Personal Memoirs*. Fawcett.

Hansen, Harry, *The Civil War*. Meredith, 1962.

Hassler, Warren W. Jr., *General George B. McClellan, Shield of the Union*. Louisiana State University Press, 1957.

*Henderson, G.F.R., *Stonewall Jackson and the American Civil War*. David McKay, 1936.

Jones, Virgil Carrington, *The Civil War at Sea*. Holt, Rinehart & Winston; I Blockaders, 1960; II River War, 1961; III Final Effort, 1962.

Lewis, Lloyd, *Sherman, Fighting Prophet*. Harcourt, Brace & World, 1958.

O'Connor, Richard, *Thomas: Rock of Chickamauga*. Prentice-Hall, 1948.

Porter, Horace, *Campaigning with Grant* (ed. by Wayne C. Temple). Indiana University Press, 1961.

Thomas, Benjamin P. and Harold M. Hyman, *Stanton: The Life & Times of Lincoln's Secretary of War*. Knopf, 1962.

Vandiver, Frank E., *Mighty Stonewall*. McGraw-Hill, 1957.

Williams, Kenneth, *Lincoln Finds a General*. (5 vols.). Macmillan, 1959.

*Williams, T. Harry, *P.G.T. Beauregard: Napoleon in Gray*. Louisiana State University Press, 1955.

Williams, T. Harry, *Lincoln and His Generals*. Knopf, 1952.

THE RECONSTRUCTION ERA (CHAPTERS 5, 6)

Beale, Howard K., *The Critical Year: A Study of Andrew Johnson and Reconstruction*. Frederick Ungar, 1958.

Bentley, George R., *A History of the Freedmen's Bureau*. University of Pennsylvania Press, 1955.

Brodie, Fawn M., *Thaddeus Stevens, Scourge of the South*. Norton, 1959.

*Chesnut, Mary Boykin, *A Diary from Dixie* (ed. by I. Martin and M. L. Avary). Peter Smith, 1961.

Coulter, Ellis Merton, *The South During Reconstruction*. Louisiana State University Press, 1947.

Daniels, Jonathan, *Prince of Carpetbaggers*. Lippincott, 1958.

DuBois, William E. B., *Black Reconstruction in America*. Russell & Russell, 1955.

*Franklin, John Hope, *Reconstruction After the Civil War*. University of Chicago Press, 1961.

Galloway, John D., *The First Transcontinental Railroad*. Simmons-Boardman, 1950.

Hesseltine, William B., and David L. Smiley, *The South in American History*. Prentice-Hall, 1960.

McKitrick, Eric L., *Andrew Johnson and Reconstruction*. University of Chicago Press, 1960.

Monaghan, Jay, *The Life of General George Armstrong Custer*. Little, Brown, 1959.

Pike, James, *The Prostrate State*. Loring and Mussey, 1935.

*Sandburg, Carl, *Abraham Lincoln, The War Years* (Vol. IV). Harcourt, Brace & World, 1954.

Schmitt, Martin F., and Dee Brown, *Fighting Indians of the West*. Scribner's, 1955.

Shenton, James P., *Reconstruction*. G. P. Putnam, 1963.

Shugg, Roger, *Origins of Class Struggle in Louisiana*. Claitor's Book Store, 1939.

Simkins, Francis B. and Robert H. Woody, *South Carolina during Reconstruction*. University of North Carolina Press, 1931.

Stryker, Lloyd K., *Andrew Johnson: A Study in Courage*. Macmillan, 1936.

Trowbridge, John T., *The Negro in Mississippi 1865-1890*. University of North Carolina Press, 1947.

THE GRANT ADMINISTRATION (CHAPTER 7)

Binkley, Wilfred E., *American Political Parties: Their Natural History*. Knopf, 1962.

*Buck, Solon J., *The Granger Movement*. University of Nebraska Press, 1963.

*Catton, Bruce, *U. S. Grant and the American Military Tradition*. Little, Brown, 1954.

Davidson, Marshall, *Life in America* (2 vols.). Houghton Mifflin, 1951.

Hesseltine, William B., *Ulysses S. Grant: Politician*. Frederick Ungar, 1957.

*Josephson, Matthew, *The Politicos*. Harcourt, Brace & World, 1938.

Mitchell, Stewart, *Horatio Seymour of New York*. Harvard University Press, 1938.

Nevins, Allan, *The Emergence of Modern America: 1867-1878*. Macmillan, 1928.

Nevins, Allan, *Hamilton Fish: The Inner History of the Grant Administration* (2 vols.). Frederick Ungar, 1957.

Paine, Albert B., *Thomas Nast: His Period and his Pictures*. Harper & Row, 1904.

Schlesinger, Arthur, *The Rise of the City: 1878-1898*. Macmillan, 1933.

Seitz, Don C., *The Dreadful Decade*. Bobbs-Merrill, 1926.

Sharkey, Robert P., *Money, Class & Party*. Johns Hopkins Press, 1959.

Van Deusen, Glyndon, *Horace Greeley: Nineteenth Century Crusader*. University of Pennsylvania Press, 1953.

Werner, M. R., *Tammany Hall*. Doubleday, Doran, 1928.

White, Leonard D., *The Republican Era: 1869-1901*. Macmillan, 1958.

*Woodward, C. Vann, *Reunion and Reaction*. Peter Smith, 1961.

ACKNOWLEDGMENTS

The author wishes to thank the following for their assistance: Dr. Thomas L. Brasher, Professor of English, Southwest Texas State College; Everette Swinney, Assistant Professor of History, Southwest Texas State College; Roy D. Smith, Industrial Training Institute, Chicago, Ill.; and E. B. Long, Oak Park, Ill. The editors of this book are particularly indebted to the following persons and institutions: James P. Shenton, Associate Professor of History, Columbia University;

Mrs. Mary Hoffman Forbes, Registrar, The Corcoran Gallery of Art, Washington, D.C.; J. Harcourt Givens, Head, Manuscript Department, The Historical Society of Pennsylvania, Philadelphia; Milton Kaplan and Carl Stange, Library of Congress, Washington, D.C.; Felix Kuntz, New Orleans, La.; Boston Museum of Fine Arts, Boston, Mass.; The Valentine Museum, Richmond, Va.; Virginia Historical Society, Richmond, Va.; and Judy Higgins.

PICTURE CREDITS

The sources for the illustrations in this book are shown below. Credits for pictures from left to right are separated by semicolons, top to bottom by dashes. Sources have been abbreviated as follows:
Bettmann—The Bettmann Archive; Brown—Brown Brothers; Culver—Culver Pictures; LC—Library of Congress;
N-YHS—The New-York Historical Society, N.Y.C.; NYPL—The New York Public Library

CHAPTER 1: 6—McLellan Lincoln Collection, Brown University Library. 8, 9—Sy Seidman; Culver. 10—Culver. 11—Bettmann—Brown. 12, 13—Bettmann; Culver—Culver; Bettmann. 14, 15—Bettmann. 16—Culver. 17—Illustrations by Charles W. Reed from *Hardtack and Coffee* by John D. Billings, published by Willard Small, Boston. 18, 19—Culver; courtesy LC. 20, 21—*Harper's Weekly;* Derek Bayes, courtesy James Higginson Weekes, Celbridge, County Kildare, Ireland. 22, 23—Ken Schmid, courtesy Mrs. Alexander McWilliams; Eric Schaal, Yale University Art Gallery, gift of Samuel R. Betts—The Metropolitan Museum of Art, gift of Mrs. Frank B. Porter, 1922; Ken Schmid, the collection of The Detroit Institute of Arts. 24, 25—Herbert Orth, courtesy of The Cooper Union Museum; Herbert Orth, New Britain Museum of American Art. 26, 27—Herbert Orth, collection of Mr. and Mrs. Norman B. Woolworth; Herbert Orth, courtesy Mr. and Mrs. Nathan Shaye—Courtesy of the Fogg Art Museum, Harvard University; courtesy Christian A. Zabriskie and Museum of Fine Arts, Boston. 28, 29—Left: Herbert Orth, courtesy Museum of Fine Arts, Boston—Herbert Orth, The Metropolitan Museum of Art, gift of Mrs. William F. Milton, 1923; right: Herbert Orth, courtesy of The Cooper Union Museum.

CHAPTER 2: 30—Valentine Museum, Richmond, Va., Conrad Wise Chapman Collection. 33—Culver. 34—U. S. Army photograph. 35—*Harper's Weekly.* 36, 37—Bettmann except right courtesy LC. 39—Courtesy American Heritage Publishing Co., Inc. 40, 41—U. S. Navy photograph; Johnson Collection, Philadelphia. 42, 43—Culver; The Whaling Museum, New Bedford, Mass.—Albert Shaw Jr. 44, 45—Painting by Tom Lovell—courtesy LC; Culver. 46, 47—Courtesy of Peabody Museum of Salem, and American Heritage Publishing Co., Inc.—courtesy of The Harvard College Library; courtesy of Confederate Museum, Richmond, Va., and American Heritage Publishing Co., Inc. 48, 49—Wadsworth Atheneum, Hartford, courtesy American Heritage Publishing Co., Inc.

CHAPTER 3: 50—Herbert Orth, painting hanging in the home of Mr. and Mrs. Charles J. Sinnott, New Orleans, La. 55—Smithsonian Institution National Air Museum. 57—Bettmann—Culver. 58, 59—Courtesy LC; Valentine Museum, Richmond, Va. 61—Culver. 63—Culver. 65—Bettmann—Culver. 66, 67—Courtesy LC. 68, 69—Photo no. 292-CV-304 in the National Archives; the National Archives—From the records of the Corps of Engineers, National Archives Record Group No. 77; U.S. Signal Corps No. 111-B-507, Brady Collection in the National Archives. 70, 71—Courtesy LC. 72, 73—Courtesy LC except top right N-YHS. 74, 75—Courtesy LC except top right photo no. 165-C-892 (right) in the National Archives. 76, 77—Courtesy LC. 78, 79—Courtesy the National Archives.

CHAPTER 4: 80—Fernand Bourges, Putnam County Historical Society. 63—Chestnut St., Cold Spring, N. Y. 82—Bettmann. 84, 85—Courtesy LC. 86, 87—Culver except right courtesy LC. 88—Culver. 90, 91—Courtesy LC. 92, 93—Sy Seidman; Valentine Museum, Richmond, Va., Conrad Wise Chapman Collection. 94, 95—Kennedy Galleries, New York. 96—New York State Historical Association, Cooperstown—Sy Seidman. 97 through 101—Courtesy LC. 102, 103—Courtesy American Heritage Publishing Co., Inc.—Kennedy Galleries, New York. 104, 105—Courtesy LC. 106, 107—Reproduced through courtesy of the Virginia Historical Society. 108—Courtesy of Tennessee Historical Society.

CHAPTER 5: 110, 111, 112—Courtesy LC. 113, 114, 115—Bettmann. 116, 117—Bettmann except bottom left Culver. 118, 119—Culver; photo no. 165-C-776 in the National Archives. 120, 121—Eric Schaal, courtesy Felix Kuntz, New Orleans, La. 122, 123—Left: Giles County Public Library, Pulaski, Tenn.; center: Culver—Bettmann; right: courtesy Louisiana State Museum. 124, 125—Culver: courtesy Abby Aldrich Rockefeller Folk Art Collection, Williamsburg, Va.

CHAPTER 6: 126—The Harry T. Peters Collection, Museum of the City of New York. 128—Culver. 130, 131—Culver. 132—NYPL-Schomberg Collection—Culver. 133—Bettmann. 134, 135—Bettmann except top right Culver. 136, 137—Culver except top right Bettmann. 138, 139—Union Pacific Railroad Photo; Herbert Orth, *The Song of the Talking Wire* by Henry F. Farny (detail), The Taft Museum, Cincinnati, Ohio. 140, 141—Left: The Society of California Pioneers; right: Wide World Photos—George Eastman House. 142, 143—Henry H. Baskerville, photo from Smithsonian Institution. 144, 145—Left: Photo no. 77-HQ-264-809 in the National Archives; right: Denver Public Library, Western Collection, photo by David F. Barry—photo no. 77-HQ-264-847 in the National Archives; courtesy J. Leonard Jennewein. 146, 147—Courtesy Harry Shaw Newman, The Old Print Shop, Inc., N.Y.C.

CHAPTER 7: 148—Stanley T. Manzer, courtesy of The White House. 150 through 156—Culver. 157—Bettmann—Culver. 158, 159—Charles P. Mills & Son, courtesy The Historical Society of Pennsylvania, Philadelphia; Kennedy Galleries, New York City. 160, 161—*In the Land of Promise: Castle Garden* by Charles F. Ulrich in the Collection of The Corcoran Gallery of Art, Washington, D.C.—N-YHS. 162, 163—Herbert Orth, The Knoedler Galleries, New York City—The Progressive Farmer Company. 164, 165—Charles P. Mills & Son, courtesy The Historical Society of Pennsylvania except bottom right N-YHS. 166, 167—Charles P. Mills & Son, courtesy Atwater Kent Museum.

INDEX

*This symbol in front of a page number indicates a photograph or painting of the subject mentioned.

Political events of the 1861-1865 period are indexed in detail in Volume 5.

Printed in U.S.A.

XXXX

176